New Writing

An Anthology of
Poetry, Fiction, Nonfiction, Drama

The Best of Americana
http://www.americanpopularculture.com

New Writing

An Anthology of Poetry, Fiction, Nonfiction, Drama

The Best of Americana
http://www.americanpopularculture.com

Edited by Leslie Wilson

Press Americana
Hollywood   Los Angeles

Press Americana
The Press of Americana:
The Institute for the Study of American Popular Culture
7095-1240 Hollywood Boulevard, Hollywood, CA 90028
http://www.americanpopularculture.com

Copyright 2013 Americana and Individual Authors

This book contains works of fiction, products of the author's imagination. Any relation to actual character, place, incident, or any other matter is purely coincidental.

Library of Congress Cataloging-in-Publication Data

New writing : an anthology of poetry, fiction, nonfiction, drama : the best of Americana / edited by Leslie Wilson.
pages cm
Includes bibliographical references and index.
ISBN 978-0-9829558-6-4 (alk. paper)
1. American literature. 2. United States--Literary collections. I. Wilson, Leslie, 1967- editor of compilation.
PS507.N49 2013
810.8'006--dc23
2013025882

TABLE OF CONTENTS

POETRY

Alexandra Ashford
West Cape   1
Lessons in Lavender   3

Peter Neil Carroll
Horse Creek, 1846   4

Darren Demaree
Emily as a Yielding   4

William Doreski
December Entropies   5
Soups of the Day   6

Donna J. Gelagotis Lee
Fit   8
Exercise   9

Howie Good
The Roofers   10
Whom Pain Has Brought to
Despair But Not Yet to Death   10

Richard Hoffman
Ars   11

William Hudson
Expectorants   12

Donald Levin
New Year's Tangerine   12

Mary MacGowan
Rowing Lessons   14

Kelly Moffett
Mourning   15

Rich Murphy
The Law and the Crooked   15
Human Resources Department   16

Jacqueline K. Powers
Alone   17

J.R. Solonche
A Young Poet and an Old Poet   18

Ann Walters
Eating Crow   19

FICTION

Rosebud Ben-Oni
The Whims of Gulls   20

J.J. Clark
The Present Perfect   31

Alan Davis
French Milled Soap   37

Roger Real Drouin
Gray   42

Katherine L. Holmes
An Elderly Woman and an Adolescent   49

Eleanor Swanson
Stray Dogs   71

NONFICTION

Donald Dewey
Blind Newsy Sees   81

Richard Thieme
I Remember Mama   90

Curtis Smith
A Rusty Chain   99

DRAMA

David-Matthew Barnes
It's a Pleasure to Be Sad   107

Timothy Braun
Las Vegas Girl   121

Jason Visconti
Dust and Doodads   129

Preface

This anthology represents some of the best creative writing submitted to Americana: An Institute for American Studies and Creative Writing at http://www.americanpopularculture.com over the last several years, which includes the work published by Press Americana, *Review Americana: A Creative Writing Journal*, Hollywood Books International, and The Poetry Press. Other pieces appear here for the first time.

Americana is a nonprofit institute dedicated to education through the publication of the best in American Studies and creative writing that reveals the truth about American culture, history, and human experience. We believe creative writers are as important as our historians in terms of examining, recording, and understanding important cultural moments. We also believe that there exists no better record of the history of America and Americans than in our culture. There we will find the hopes, needs, dreams, desires, and struggles of the people. Through the careful analysis of our twentieth and twenty-first century American history and culture, we can more clearly understand where we have been and who we have been and thus consciously consider where we want to go, who we want to be, how we want to live, and what public policies we want to endorse as twenty-first century Americans. This process will help us formulate our identities and find our ideological and spiritual direction.

We hope you enjoy these writers as much as we have. This anthology works as a fundraiser for Americana so that we may continue to offer publishing opportunities to writers such as those represented on these pages. Above all, we want to thank them for their contributions.

We also hope you'll visit us on the web at http://www.americanpopularculture.com

Leslie Wilson, Editor

POETRY

ALEXANDRA ASHFORD

West Cape

In Memoriam

This year the cape has changed.
Green is anchored deeper
than the water itself.
Sky looks so much like sea
even the egrets are confused,

just the way you'd want it.

I spent this winter envisioning you
back at the vineyard, fingers sticky
with "blueberry surprise,"
back glued to the longest branch
of white-blooded birch.

I am twelve again
waiting for you to run into
the meadow, that Cheshire
Cat of a smile on your face,
so we can race to that cliff
on the north end, the one with
vines and foxgloves covering
the lighthouse, whitewashed and grand
against a distance of gunmetal blue.

It was there that we laughed until
our stomachs hurt, took our
first sips of moonshine

(my uncle's brew)
smashed fireflies and rubbed
our skin sore so that we too might
glow.
That was years before the deacons
clothed in black. The summer
covered in moths, weeds,
cicadas. The cemetery singing:

Your loss is my gain.

At the west end of this square
a headstone floraled, faded
and dreaming. Your name
etched deliberately into
stone. Years curved in calligraphy:

1984-2005

The small line between
years meant to symbolize
a whole life: the boy who shared my
summers draped in magic.
As if you were no vaster
than that small space
between the years, the life you lived
little more than language
unfolding itself on a rock.

Lessons in Lavender

Lavender sugar and primrose
spread out on the table.
You used it for everything:
to kill the cat smell in the carpet,
in the lotion to make it pop.
Your wedding dress was purple
and so is the gown
you were buried in.
It was ageless
on your body,
a rim around the moon
sugar plum shadow,
Tchaikovsky at Christmas time—
the year mama wore the purple chiffon
and looked flawless.
You had dreamed of fish
and losing a tooth:
a birth
and a death.
We ate neckbones and black eyed peas
for luck,
then after dark
you boiled the lavender.
The house smelled too much
of chaos, you said,
so much coming and going.

For more work from Alexandra Ashford, look for her collection *Danke Schoen* from The Poetry Press of Press Americana.

PETER NEIL CARROLL

Horse Creek, 1846

Laughing Lakota girls and boys
splash in the cool waters,
scream with delight.

A nearly naked man holds
a white horse by a loose cord,
fixes his gaze on the procession
of canvas-covered wagons,
slow and heavy
crossing the shallow creek.

The wheels cut into dry prairie
grass, severing the roots. As far
as the horizon, he sees the wound
harden into a wide brown trail.

For more work from Peter Neil Carroll, look for his collection *A Child Turns Back to Wave: Poetry of Lost Places* from The Poetry Press of Press Americana.

DARREN DEMAREE

Emily as a Yielding

Soft laughter, hope
that the mouth suffers
only because the mind

has limited the austerity
measures, that elegy
has been vanquished

& this morning raises
the field, the flower,
the broad desires

of a girl named Emily,
my woman named Emily,
who is of the field

& over the field
& possibly the mad sun
that echoes harvesting.

WILLIAM DORESKI

December Entropies

Snowshoeing through lumbered hills
I detect a fresh terror
in deer tracks that stumble through drifts

and leap and land splay-footed
on modest slopes where cut boughs rot
under two feet of cover.

I slip-shoe down to the Mill Brook
and trudge along its frozen surface
to explore the beaver pond built

last summer. The lodge, a mass
of snow as tall as me, resists
imaginings evinced by fox-tracks

all over the dome. The beavers,
unintimidated, doze
for the winter, recalling the roar

of chainsaws that competed
with their own tree-felling skills.
Come spring they'll find the pond

where they left it, fox and snowshoe
tracks erased, surviving pines
garnishing indifferent sky.

The sky lacks indifference today,
however. Snow-showers whisper
into the void, and the light fails

early. Tramping home in the dusk
I feel the distance attenuate
while my snowshoe-tracks describe me

a creature so long obsolete
that the cruelest of biographies
can't even begin to exhume me.

Soups of the Day

In blue and white flower-print dress
you look as meager as a handshake.
Around us the city rumbles
as evening yawns above the river.

Dazzled by displays of silk and gold,
we stalk through a department store
and exit into a lamplit square.
You're starving and eager to expend

your appetite at the coffee shop
behind the museum. Shadows bend
around corners and pool so deeply
we could drown if we aren't careful.

But the coffee shop's bright enough
to compete with Descartes or Hegel
so we sit at the counter and choose
among the many soups of the day.

Tomato cheddar, chicken and rice.
Our choices divide us. We eat
with clear conscience, yet you
in that scrawny dress seem alien

and oblique, and I want to dodge
through the kitchen and exit
into the alley where the simper
of hungry rats would sicken you.

Meanwhile you'd rise and fly away
with that evil dress blooming
about you, and your cruel pale laugh
would feel those fragile citizens

emerging from the museum
warped by Monet's tender pastels.
We finish our soups and agree
they brew good broth here. The night

has settled in to stay so we split
at the door, you catching a bus
to your suburban hideaway
where spouse and children deploy,

and me walking six blocks north
to a sublet with view of smokestacks
no longer functioning. The river
sloughs along. A thunder of bats

folds and unfolds two hundred feet
overhead, and I'll sport the scar
of your sisterly kiss until
the fresh dawn washes it off.

DONNA J. GELAGOTIS LEE

Fit

I lean on the windowsill
to bite a cloud as it passes by.

Now, I feel the city on my breath,
taste its pungent odor,

its hard edges of steel,
chrome mirrors of sunlight,

the rough ledges of its
architecture skipping over

my tongue. In the stark
relentless realism of a business

day, I hunt like an animal
the long tail of adventure.

I want to grab it, swing it
around in the air, like

King Kong in Manhattan,
everything toy and miniature.

Exercise

I am pulling my yellow band
over Brooklyn, where the hospital
and high-rise buildings post
signs in Russian. I am catching
the city light as it spits
out the soot history
toils in, sunlight gleaming
in the window of a bakery,
on the black rim
of a Hassidic Jew's hat,
the Hanukkah menorah
six days lit and strung
to the top of a Chevy
while Jewish men and boys
dance in the landscaped
park of a mini strip mall,
their faces white
as pancake powder.
I am chewing on a latke
the baker Samuel handed me
for free, folded
in a white napkin
like a present, his yarmulke
the round reminder
of belief that does not stray.
I am standing over Brooklyn,
recalling my grandfather,
from Kiev, strolling the boardwalk
with a rolled *Pravda*
under his arm. I have taken

the width of this borough
in my grasp and am stretching it,
feeling its strength.
I am at home, the wide
borough of a country relaxing
in a natural reflex.

HOWIE GOOD

The Roofers

for Gabriel

It isn't the meaning
of these words
that matters
just the sound
like the hammering
from next door
a couple of roofers
on their knees
and racing the light
because it may be true
what they heard
tomorrow rain

Whom Pain Has Brought to Despair But Not Yet to Death

If this was a movie, I'd be chased down a dark alley, find a body in my hotel room, get ridiculed when I told the police what I knew or at least suspected. But it's not, the morning light the approximate putty color of dull pain. Something knocks twice upon my heart without entering. I give up trying to go back to sleep. Clio, goddess of history, drinking her coffee from a skull mug downstairs, looks forward to a future very like the past.

For more work from Howie Good, look for his collection *Lovesick* from The Poetry Press of Press Americana.

RICHARD HOFFMAN

Ars

Yes, but
the hammer
was made for the nail,

the plane to shave,
the chisel to hew,

and the drill although
in any gauge
exquisite is not curled to please

so speak to me
of our common work
and like the wood,
like the stone,
I will listen.

WILLIAM HUDSON

Expectorants

Words spew sometimes
Like a spasm come unclenched

Or they seep out slow
As pus from an unscabbed wound,
Or flow like blood,

Bright, pulsing red
With lust or joy.

But most often
They hic-hic-hic
In staccato
Little bursts

As though, with a series
Of hacking coughs,
We seek to expel
Them like peanut hulls
Stuck back in our throats.

DONALD LEVIN

New Year's Tangerine

I peel off the tough resisting skin
of the dense globe
that weights the hollow of my hand
and spread it on the plate
like a mercator projection

and think of my father
when his small frame bent
over the dining room table
as he separated the wedges
of his own small fruit

into a careful flower
each crisp slice red orange
full and refreshing
like a wall of water bags
hung on a fence, the juice

spilling down his chin
while he noisily sucked up
the pulp, so innocent seeming
until it blocked his system
that first new night of the year

so long ago, knowing
he shouldn't eat these
while he drained the delicious
flavor of one, then another,
then a third sliver, the sweet taste

urging him on toward the hospital
where we rushed him, the urgency
of his need for tangerine sugar
for once defeating the wild force
of his untamable caution.

MARY MACGOWAN

Rowing Lessons

My mother said,
You must sit backwards
to row a boat.
Pick a tree across the way,
hold it on twelve o'clock
behind you, before you
that's how you must steer
from the boat's center.

My father said,
Push down through air
up through water.
Watch your tree
fall away, even when
you feel like you're
drawing it closer
with every pull.

I've learned that
now and then
you can sneak a look
behind you
to see what's ahead
which is always arriving.
But mostly they were right,
everything falls away
in spite of you
because of you.

KELLY MOFFETT

Mourning

At the earliest sounds of spring
In March, a tinny flop from the mail slot
Seems like a sound in my mouth,
A tongue's click.

And the mail lady's hand
A memory of all senses
Reaching into my house.
That tin cry—It was like

A new understanding of how
The news sinks in.

An open shove through,
Then a slamming shut.

RICH MURPHY

The Law and the Crooked

An Atonement festival twists television
cameras into faces, quarters slums
and trailer parks. Only after police
pour light into the alleys and citizens
carve patriotism into county jails,
legend owns the turf and promotes
from within. Dragnets sweep corners
to streets for facts but leave riffraff
behind. The vigilantes envision
glory and so hear sirens screeching

as lacking enough agony from culprits.
In past centuries, pikes and the panopticon
taught little where a trio – prosecutor,
persecutor, and prey – each pled
for something different. The gift
that keeps on giving the fun
that creates its own sun echoes
with memory let loose on screens.

Human Resources Department

Mining human resources,
The Cranium and Ligament
Exploitation Corporation saps
consciousness while drilling
for energy. Lights switch on
around the world but short out
enlightenment to dim wit
headlamps, while a double chain
scraper conveyor boom cleans
lifetimes and wallets
for headquarters incorporated.
In the end, the brilliance
for the tunnel boring machine
strips away from the sides
personhood embedded
in psyches, rendering
freedom unnecessary.
The Division for Coercion—
rewards and punishments—
carves holes and right angles
through talents and intellects
day in and day out until
the grateful stick figure flops
beneath a flower bed.

For more work from Rich Murphy, look for his collection *Americana* from The Poetry Press of Press Americana.

JACQUELINE K. POWERS

Alone

Despite or because –
not an island, exactly, though
you say I live too much inside myself.
Perhaps a peninsula,
a cautious jutting forth.

We watch a speckled fawn
under the apple tree, feet splayed.
A hummingbird's
rapid-fire assaults on red plastic.

Gymnastic squirrels
inadvertently shake birdseed
to the ground and a trio of wild turkeys,
the painted tuft
of a red-crested lucy bird.

Silence like waves through water –
then humid-heavy birdsong.
Later a full moon, garish
as a clown's face
but I can just about breathe again.

For more work from Jacqueline K. Powers, look for her collection *The Mysteries of Fishing and Flight* from The Poetry Press of Press Americana.

J.R. SOLONCHE

A Young Poet and an Old Poet

A young poet brought some poems he had written to an old poet he respected. The poems were full of airy sentiments, vagueness and philosophical generalities. The old poet read the poems with patience. Every so often he made a barely audible humming sound. Then he gave the poems back to the young poet and said, *A poem must have a body as well as a soul.* The young poet went home to his room where he tore up the poems. He put the pieces in a bowl. Then he wrote new poems, which, on the next day, he brought to the old poet he respected. These new poems were full of very specific details, the names of things both natural and man-made, and much matter-of-factness. The old poet read the poems with patience. Every so often he made a barely audible humming sound. Then he gave the poems back to the young poet and said, A *poem must have a soul as well as a body.* The young poet went home to his room where he tore up the poems. He put the pieces in the bowl that held the pieces of the old poems he had torn up. He mixed the pieces together and spilled them out onto the table. He glued the pieces together and the next day brought them to the old poet he respected. The old poet did not have to read the poems because he could see what the young poet had done. He saw that pieces did not fit. He said, *A poem must have a body and a soul with no space or seam between them.* The young poet was despondent. He went home and threw the poems in the river. A year later, while walking by the shore of the ocean, the young poet saw something in the water. He bent over and picked it up. It was a shell with paper inside. On the paper was written a poem. The young poet brought it to the old poet he respected. The old poet read the poem and right away said, *This is a poem. Hang it out on a pine branch to dry.*

ANN WALTERS

Eating Crow

You don't mind
the feathers.
They tickle at first
and only hurt later
when the quills
pierce your gut.

The beak is loud
but harmless
and the eyes are easy
as long as you don't
meet their stare.

It's the feet
that make you gag,
that stick in your throat
until you cough up
toe after toe
filthy with pride.

FICTION

ROSEBUD BEN-ONI

The Whims of Gulls

For M.E. Parker

That same day the bridge was blown up by Border Patrol, a peculiar flock of seagulls descended upon the high desert town of Marfa. From the window of his bedroom on the second floor, Joaquín watched twenty or so gulls crisscross the overcast sky, calling out to each other in growing alarm. At least five hundred miles from the Gulf of Mexico, he couldn't understand what would bring them here. Surely something had led them astray.

The wind was harsh that August evening, a sweeping ferocity that slapped the screen door against the paint-chipped siding. An indistinct grey rolled above, erupting with patches of muted lightning. Usually these kinds of unfavorable conditions would've sent him in search of little Paola, who'd disappear in the tall clumps of switchgrass and black dalea shrubs that now grew wild and unfettered all over the former ranch. Joaquín always knew how to find her, tracking for signs until he saw the bees scatter among the shrubs. He'd listen for the rocky soil crunching beneath the thin soles of her plastic sandals as she crept across on her haunches; the sound oddly comforted him. Stopping at a distance, just far enough for his voice to carry over through the tall grass, he'd announce that he would count to ten; usually around nine, her little head would pop up and she'd give him a toothy grin.

But that evening after Joaquín collected her, he hadn't insisted that she come inside, only that she stay on the porch until dinnertime. She'd pecked him on the cheek as he put her down, and then slipped off her sandals as she'd climbed up on the porch swing. Instead of heading to the kitchen, he'd fled to his study, feeling a migraine coming on as the winds died down and the mugginess crept into the house. He'd opened the window and waited for the wind to return.

After an hour, the wetness bore down on him. His vision became fuzzy and what lay before seemed to be boiling, and for a moment, he drowned in the deadness of his own thoughts, forgetting where he was. Rubbing his temples, he listened to Paola pushing off the ground with her bare feet, the tarnished metal chains creaking. She was now heavy enough so that the uneven rods, which suspended its weight lifted up on one side, tilting her slightly.

It would be dark soon, the weak light of the evening sun escaping from just beneath the horizon. But just as he arose to call her inside, one of the gulls veered away from the rest. It flew low over a long patch of cacti and bluebonnets that grew on both sides of the steel fence separating his property from the Interstate. The throbbing between his eyes quickened as it sailed toward him, and a sudden chill swept through the air, stirring the evening from its stupor, lifting the somnolent land from the heaviness of the humidity. He felt the wind of his face as the gull curved past his open window and then flew straight up into the air with a direct precision that left him breathless.

Thunder rumbled across the haze, and for a moment the gull seemed to stop short right in the air, hanging onto a sudden gust. Joaquín rubbed his eyes; perhaps it was a hallucination brought on by an aura of the migraine. But as the wind grew stronger, the gull was knocked back and tumbled from the sky, zigzagging as if falling down some unseen staircase, belly-up, its wings twisted at the ends.

Just as Joaquín arose from his chair, so that he could see where it would land, a horrible screech rang out as its contorted body collided with a battered pickup that was pulling up onto the driveway, just outside the new gate of his home.

Slamming on its brakes, the truck stopped quickly as the gull slowly slid off the hood of the truck. His mouth went dry, and he felt his skin warm. After a moment, the engine revved, though the truck did not come any closer. Joaquín watched as the bird fell to the ground and hobbled away, the clattering sound sharpening into a stammer, the pulse of transmission quicker than that which beat on the left side of his head. It was a sound he remembered from years ago: the sound of false hesitation.

So she had come after all; Joaquín rarely remembered her making good on a promise. When she had called earlier in the week, he'd tried not to take it as an insult when, after ten years in passing now, she'd asked if he was still living in Sal Si Puedes.

Daddy had said never to come back, and even today I still hear Mamma going on that I shouldn't push the issue, when it was my old double-cab, my stupid suitcase with faded daffodils, my wrenching and yanking like I knew what was at stake when they locked me inside the truck, still half-delirious from the complications. I sat between them the entire way, so we all saw where I was going, clear as day. No one said a word from there on – I never had been caught in such stillness. Like all the hope in the world had been caught on the curve of the wind, sailed right over our heads, just missing the thorns of our ancient mesquite tree where Mamma and Daddy had been fighting and I had been wrenching and yanking, and suddenly we all stopped. And I mean like we all went into collective heart failure, as what had gone haywire and tongue-wild in the air that day suddenly went quiet, dead and right. Like how the first autumn northerners barrel in out of nowhere, just to hurl themselves straight into stillness.

In his youth, Leigh Davis had been the headache of her family. Her inquisitive nature and flighty behavior were forgiven by other girls due to her lack of beauty. At fourteen, Leigh was stick-thin, with an angular face and pale skin that looked wrong with the frosted makeup popular at the time. She didn't tease her hair, which was too straight to perm, nor did she lay claims to any boys, and for both these shortcomings, she was immensely popular. Most mothers simply felt sorry for her, for a woman so young to understand the limits of what she could acquire.

However, things changed when Leigh showed up to make her debut at Junior Cotillion in a flamenco dress instead of proper taffeta with a sweetheart neckline. Her mother was the only mother who hadn't shown up, and the ladies of Marfa couldn't blame her.

They watched in horror as their daughters rushed up to her, fingering the silk fan and marveling at the Spanish comb that held the bun high on her head.

Wasn't Leigh Davis old enough to know better, they whispered to each other, all the while smiling politely. *Or was she taking advantage of her well-respected father's well-known financial problems, which left him little time to worry about anything else?*

All would've been forgiven for such an awkward, gangly girl, until the future star quarterback asked her to dance. One mother waited for them to dance by to announce that perhaps Leigh Davis would rather find herself living on the other side of the river.

When Joaquín heard this story three years later, he'd asked her if that was where she got the idea to be with him.

For she'd then bloomed into a full-on spectacle, spending money her family no longer had on turquoise jewelry, long denim dresses and tall boots with suede fringe. Her father had refused to acknowledge any of this when he'd drive into town every Friday, just before sunrise. He was a tall man in tight jeans with a bit of a gut over his belt, with a gait slow and straight, as if he had yard sticks stuck in his pants legs, his arm arched at his sides in perfect right angles. He'd stop off at the Firebird Diner for coffee and the latest troubles: feuds along the border, never enough rain, disappointing sales at livestock auctions. He always listened and advised, but never offered up his own lamentations.

After collecting his mail, he'd then make the rounds at the stores as if it was his official duty to check in on their well-being. But as his finances diminished and her ensembles became more absurd, he ventured into town less often, sending a ranch hand instead to run his errands.

Joaquín had never met her father and wondered how much he knew about them. What had Davis said, for instance, when his daughter commissioned a seamstress from Sal Si Puedes to make her pleated skirts with lace, in homage to those once worn by Joaquín's mother's family, who had descended from the Mazahua women of Michoacán. His mother, who wore shorts and t-shirts, had never taken kindly to Leigh doing this, nor did the families of ranchers who were soon facing foreclosure and bankruptcy, just like the Davis family.

After Davis lost the property, which was bought by an oil man who'd come to retire and play cowboy, he moved his family to nearby, tiny Candelaria. Though defeated, he never stopped rebuilding the lines that had so clearly defined him. In fact, he was the first one who'd proposed the removal of the rickety footbridge between Candelaria and the Mexican farming village of San Antonio. He warned the townspeople of the burgeoning number of Mexicans who freely crossed over, that they did not come for Candelaria, but had their sight set on taking over Marfa, its houses, its schools, its city council.

Over two decades later, now that the drug trade was out of control, Davis had his wish granted. But he'd died just days before he could see the bridge was destroyed, as border patrol trucks rolled in and left behind not one piece of the wood or wire, the murky water of the river below motionless, coursing nowhere along either side of the muddy banks.

Daddy promised the stillness wouldn't be real once I got real problems. In Plano, before they left me for good, he said, Leigh, if you're smart, you'll forget the stillness inside and the broken bits left behind and never look for the why. Cause all you gonna find is the bitter sums when the sky tries to add up the land beneath it.

Years later, though, the stillness has grown, sprouted roots, deep and twisted. I keep thinking about the nomads who'd settled Candelaria, all the time they had to themselves. And I wonder if nomads knew time at all. I'd like to think they didn't.

I'd like to think there was a time when everything was anything, so your road would've been my road. That is, straight to the water source. When there were no strangers, just new things. And so much in the world was far from plain and clear, but that was no big deal.

No one knew much about Candelaria, not even Joaquín's father who knew everything about the border. He'd told his son that nomads had settled the town, though he couldn't say why they chose the area. The old man had never liked Candelaria and thought it was for failures and smugglers.

Joaquín's family had lived for three generations on the poorer side of Marfa, in an unofficial *colonia* that the residents called Sal Si Puedes. Most of the adobe houses had no plumbing, and it wasn't until Joaquín had left for college in Austin that the *colonia* finally had a paved street.

Leigh had had two minds about him going to college. At that time, someone like Joaquín didn't have much of a future in Marfa; his intelligence and drive would've been wasted. But she was bitter all the same, for while he was getting out, she was being driven further in: Davis was doing his best to marry her off to one of the sons of the many oil men now flooding Marfa.

While she was being presented to middle-aged men in proper taffeta with sweetheart necklines, Joaquín spent much of that summer alone, wandering the area around the Caldera rim. He didn't see Leigh at all until the night before she called just as he was going to sleep. She wanted him to go to a motel with her in Alpine, where no one would know them.

What he remembered most was the silence that then fell between them, and how they'd spent most of the time in that open shower. The metallic taste of the droplets of water stuck to her face, as her slight body pushed him hard up against the wall, the peeling wallpaper sticking to his back. They'd both slipped, several times, but wouldn't stop until they physically couldn't.

They collapsed on the bed, the comforter smelling of stale smoke, with wet hair, the towels drawn tight at their waists. The bed was never unmade, and they checked out an hour before the sun rose.

Joaquín drove home to Sal Si Puedes in her pickup, as she curled up in his poncho in the backseat right behind him, hunched against the window. No matter how much he adjusted his rear view mirror, he couldn't see her face.

He stopped just on the outskirts of the *colonia*, watched her sleep for a moment, and then reached out to touch her. Leigh woke up quickly, backing away from the touch that interrupted her dreams. He waited for her to collect herself and then asked if she was awake enough to drive back to Candelaria.

Leigh didn't answer him but climbed over the front seat as if they were merely switching drivers. She pulled off the poncho and tossed it to him, pushing him out of the driver's seat. She laughed as she drove off, honking until the *colonia* dogs began barking and ran out to him.

Months later, no matter how many times he washed the poncho at school, it still carried that sweaty, stale smell of the comforter, mixed with the sandalwood essence she wore. He did poorly in his class that first semester and called her every Sunday when her family was at church. He counted down the days until Christmas break.

But when he came home, she'd become engaged to the son of a now impoverished oil heir. After an argument just outside the *colonia*, which the residents of Sal Si Puedes witnessed from a distance, Joaquín and Leigh disappeared.

They camped out that night near at the stony grounds of the Sierra Vierja, and almost froze to death. Wearing only a pair of jeans and a light sweater, Joaquín covered her shivering body in the poncho, their throats filling with the cold, until they stumbled onto an abandoned barn. It was the last time they'd ever see each other. After that night, his grades improved dramatically, but the rough fibers of the poncho caused him to break out into welts, and he'd have to throw it away by next spring.

Mamma says he went out all skin and bone and free of past regrets because he no longer planned on leaving anything behind. This morning at the funeral, no one would speak to me, or sit with me in the pews, not even Mama, and during the service I thought about when her father was still alive. He'd never gotten along with Daddy and just before he died, I was the only one he'd speak to and I remember he told me that the bell of the market sounded like a carillon of church bells and people didn't know whether it was time to praise God or head over to the slaughterhouse. When the border was one big lie and the siesta was as official as things needed to be and all border-dwellers were called Tejanos whether white or brown. When life was understood as it was lived. On horseback, down the trails, along the railroads. When places and names were not set in stone, and truth roamed free as the people cause they understood that life meant to be pursued, not studied and pulled apart until all you got is facts but no hope for them.

And that next Christmas Joaquín did not come home, although it was around this time that Leigh's mother had come to call on his mother in Sal Si Puedes, cradling a screaming infant in her arms. The child was just too dark to think otherwise, Mrs. Davis had said, refusing to come inside, and leaving Joaquín's mother to raise Paolo for the first five years of her life.

His mother still liked to remind him that Paola had cost Leigh her impoverished oil heir and banished her to distant relatives in Plano. She told him, this is how her people live with us: we have literally been cleaning up their lives for years. And when it's something they don't like, they send it away and rebuild their sand-castles in the desert, when the desert will always win.

Only now Joaquín knew that his mother had been right all along; the desert was indeed encroaching and the land wasn't good anymore. Rather than face that the landscape of power had shifted in Marfa and try to adapt, those like the Davis family buried themselves further into their own illusions of right and wrong. To them, he was an illegal, an invader taking over, when he'd been born in Marfa, when his ancestors had helped build those ranches, as well as the very schools and restaurants that hadn't allowed Mexican-Americans in. As the stones of those markers now crumbled, it was up to him to clean it up – but not in the way his mother had learned. For now Joaquín, a college graduate, was on the city school board, seeking funding for outreach programs to those in the *colonias*. He did not care to disturb the old timers' delusions of grandeur: the cowboy churches, the family-owned storefronts on Main Street, the spirit of land that could not be broken anymore than the feral horses that had long since disappeared. These fantasies were to be left for them and the tourists. For those so easily fooled.

Originally, he'd come back to Marfa with the hope that Leigh would return. And yet it was for Paola that he'd leave it for a place that didn't fade along with its glory days, where the last bridge between it and somewhere else had been destroyed not out of fear but spite. No, he couldn't stay, for he was just as guilty when, rather than save what was left of the Davis family's ancient mesquite, he'd rounded up some day laborers in Candelaria. He'd sat on the porch swing for an entire afternoon, watching them uproot the centurial tree. Then he armed them with chainsaws to make it easier to cart it away to the dump.

It wasn't until this moment that Joaquín realized he'd also been seeking a larger sense of revenge. When the oil man who'd bought the Davis ranch went broke, it was Joaquín who'd seized it at a government auction at a murderously paltry sum, and then let it fall into a state of ruin. What he hadn't expected, though, was the resistance from his own parents. For all his desire to move them into a modern house, his parents chose to remain in Sal Si Puedes, in their adobe home across the hastily paved road. They couldn't bear the shame, unable to understand why someone like Joaquín who'd gotten out would come back, to where everything changed rapidly and yet remained the same, to a place stuck in a continual shattering stillness, in a long-drawn-out conflict that had never been a war but a way of life.

She held my eyes, even from a distance. I hadn't expected such eyes, so large and uneasy that they overwhelmed her small face. It was as if she'd been watching me all her life from a distance, sitting on that porch swing where Daddy used to rock himself calm, contemplating the dry scraps of his land that became more dust than soil.

I don't know how long I sat in my truck, with those big eyes on me, with those strange cries ringing out all around and the new gate tall and black and shining in the overcast. He'd put up a steel fence that stretched so far it seemed to go on forever, not at all like the rusty wire strung around the crooked fence-posts of my childhood, its wood worn both by weather and resignation, how many years did Daddy spend talking about replacing it, but said we no longer had anything worth stealing.

And, now before me, what has been taken and what has been left behind: that bruised, swaying darkness, the sound of things that lie in wait, opaque and unknown, seeming so far away and I no longer knew this place and I did not know her at all and yet had carried them both all the same, for he'd become the link between them in my absence and at that moment everything that had laid between me and them surged high above, flinging the stillness from heights both vast and slight, as if there'd never been any ground at all.

She stepped out of the battered pickup, struggling with an overstuffed suitcase, her head bowed and almost imperceptible beneath a large black hat. She wore a simple, dark dress that stopped just below the knee. It fit her tightly, but as if to emphasize a certain severity rather than the shape of her body. Was this really the same woman?

As she approached the gate, he suddenly saw that the fallen gull was trying to squeeze its body between the bars. The woman didn't seem to notice; she was looking up at him, where his study – once her father's – extended over the front porch. He wondered if she could see him, if she remembered that last desperate night in the motel, if she knew that Paola lived with him now.

As she came closer, her shadow grew long and thin in the dim light, passing right through the gull and onto the front yard that hadn't been mowed in almost a year. At that moment, he thought about little Paola who liked the state of things very much, and how each day she wandered further away from the house, deeper into the ten acres that he himself had not yet fully explored. He liked having to find her every evening just before dinner, although sometimes his heart beat wildly, and he worried that he might one day lose her that open field overrun by weeds and wildflowers.

Such displays of abandon wouldn't fool Leigh Davis, who knew what constituted neglect, and what was simply indifference.

As a rough wind stirred in the sky, inciting shriller cries from the gulls above, the woman cried out as the small figure ran toward her. She fell to one knee and held out her arms, weeping loudly enough for Joaquín to hear through the tumult, but Paola stopped short at the gate, barely paying attention to the woman. At first, he didn't understand why Paola was crouching down, ignoring the woman's cries and frantic waving of her arms.

But when he realized what Paola was doing, he too wanted to cry out. The little girl had never seen a gull before, and didn't know that once the ungrateful creature was free, it would call out to its flock and put her in danger. Imagining the soft skin of her hands being ripped open, he wanted to shout, *leave it alone*, but couldn't. All he could do was close his eyes and count to ten.

Before he was halfway, he heard the creaking sound of the gate. He opened them to see the woman motioning for him to come down, Paola's hands empty and reaching up to the sky as if she was still letting go.

But Joaquín turned away from the window. He put his head down in the desk and cried without a sound, hoping that Paola would sneak in and surprise him by touching his neck with her freezing hands, as she liked to do in the evenings.

J.J. CLARK

The Present Perfect

Lily June followed her grandfather from standpipe to standpipe as he opened valves to release the cold water onto the scorched field. Although the day dawned cool when the sun rose in the East, the same sun setting in the West on a late July afternoon was unrelenting. When Boppa stopped for a moment to dig out a clogged valve, he said, "You stay put, L.J." He worked while she sat on a levee, her tanned pot belly in full command of the space between her cutoffs and frilly pink bikini top. Boppa had once told her, "If you unscrew your bellybutton, your butt will fall off." It was a pearl of sage wisdom that she treasured. The horizon rippled and curled like a hair singed by heat, and while the temperature outside caused Lily considerable discomfort, it was preferable to the chill of her air-conditioned home on North Seventh Street. The lure of a nearby canal full of rushing water, however, was a far more tempting kind of cool, and the burbling sound convinced Lily in an instant to sneak a swim. She was quite adept at vanishing at will, and when she was sure that Boppa was good and distracted with his plugged-up cement pipe, Lily slipped away.

The water beckoned, and in mere moments she was enticed into the coolness of the grass-bottomed canal. Floating on her stomach in the murky fluid, Lily's shoulders and neck sizzled as the sun beat down on her back, but she willed herself to stay still. Her tiny body spun with the current, just another leaf adrift on its surface, and the underwater world flowed in and out of her vision. Water beetles exploded from the bottom sludge and wriggled away in search of another hideout, leaving behind slow-motion swirls of silt. When a feather of moss drifted by, found her cheek, and stuck there, she didn't blink. An awful mineral taste filled her mouth and black mosquito fish nibbled and poked at the undersides of her arms, but Lily remained quiet in spite of the discomfort, allowing the pulsating movement of the swaying pond grass to mesmerize her as she twirled motionless down the channel. The roar of the current was muted in her ears, as was the rhythmic sound of tiny bubbles escaping from her right nostril: Poink, poink, poink…

Yet she didn't stir, convinced that any motion on her part would disturb the delicate miracle that now visited her. Something had enveloped Lily completely. Something perfect. Her body skated along the top of the water like a Jesus bug, the surface tension unbroken, the water barely denting in around her form. She dared not move for fear of competing with the flow, and instead drifted along, rigid and limp all at once. Her tiny muscles were exhausted from their very calmness, from the non-effort of keeping her supine body from moving even a fraction so as not to upturn the balance she had stumbled upon. But the burden of being attached to her body soon became too much trouble for Lily, and her tether to this world gave way with a snap.

She was almost gone when she heard a man's voice from behind her, distant and frightened. Without warning, the water surged and roiled, and she found herself fighting against brown muddy waves. A huge hand clutched the back of her neck and plucked her from the water like a drenched kitten. Lily struggled, even resisted. Her feet found the bottom of the ditch, but before she could stand, she was dragged backwards out of the canal and onto the bank. She took a breath, but there was no room for air in her lungs. A hand pushed on her stomach and ditch water rushed out of her mouth and nose. She was jerked into a sitting position as she choked up fluid. Her arms were lifted above her head, and she was shook and pounded on the back so hard, she thought her lolling head was going to snap right off of her neck.

Jesus, Jesus, someone said. Lily's vision returned before her voice, and the face of her grandfather bled into focus. The man was tall and broad, and he squatted in front of her to see her eye-to-eye. She had no sooner regained her wind than the words aspirated from her mouth with her first solid exhale: "I was breathing!"

Boppa collapsed on the bank next to her and pulled a blue bandanna out of his back pocket. "Well, you seem to be now, anyway," he said. He mopped the ditchwater and sweat off of his face. He wiped his eyes, too, and blew his nose. "Why didn't I see that coming?" he asked someone, Lily didn't know who but it wasn't her.

"I was breathing underwater!" she said in a tone that insisted upon acknowledgement.

"Breathing?" he asked. She nodded, eyes wide, waiting for the look of astonishment she was sure would wash over his face. But Boppa just shook his head and some of the worried creases between his eyebrows eased up. "From where I was standing, it looked more like drowning." His eyes darkened. "Christ, don't you ever pull a stunt like that again, do you understand me?"

She nodded and bit her lower lip to keep it from trembling; it was a short journey from there to tears, and she didn't want to cry. After a moment of letting her suffer, he reached out to hug her and she didn't resist. She scooted over and rested her head on his knee, the wet denim of his Levis cool and stiff, the wrinkles forming impressions on her cheek. It was okay to cry a little now because he couldn't see, and she did cry because she knew that he didn't understand. Or he didn't believe her, which was even worse. It was because he was so *old,* she thought. Last Christmastime she told him that she wished he was a kid like her. He had fished a lariat out from underneath the seat of the pickup truck and told her that they were like different ends on a piece of rope. He stretched the rope out so that the ends were far apart, but then he grabbed both ends and brought them together in a circle. Then he tied the lariat into a hangman's noose and they played sheriff and rustler for the rest of the afternoon.

Her fine hair dried out quickly in the sun, taking on a texture and color so like straw that Lily had to be careful around Blackie and Blaze because more than once they had tried to nibble strands straight off of her scalp. With large, clumsy hands her grandfather tried to untangle the tangles her hair had made around the plastic clips holding her pigtails, picking out reeds and strings of moss while he worked. "This is easier when you're still," he mumbled, and she felt comforted.

After a long time, she said, "You don't believe me."

He was quiet for a while. Then he pinched her neck where gills would be, saying, "You're not a fish," and Lily couldn't help giggling.

"Stop it," she replied, swatting at his hands. "I was breathing underwater."

"Okay. Whatever you say." He grinned as she pouted. Spying a rock pressed into the mud bank, he leaned over to dig it out with his thumb. When he had extracted the pebble, he wiped it on the leg of his jeans and gave it to Lily.

"Pretty," she said of the dense piece of granite shot through with soft quartz. She put the rock in her pocket, and both got up and scanned the ground for more. Her very best treasures had come from Boppa. He whittled horses for her out of sticks unless she deemed a particular burl of wood too pretty to carve up with his pocket knife. Once he gave her the tail off of a muskrat he had killed, and she carried the dried out appendage around with her in her pocket, showing it off to strangers when it seemed appropriate.

They poked around the muddy bank as Holstein cattle gathered in a timid circle around the pair, too frightened to get too close, too curious to ignore the two of them entirely. Boppa found a flat, round rock, and in a fluid motion turned at the waist and skipped the stone across the ditch, his sudden movement serving to scatter the cattle with a rumble of dust. Lily and her grandfather watched as the stone bounced once, twice, three times on the surface of the water before it sank. "How does it do that?" Lily asked. "Rocks can't float."

"Who says?"

"Everyone."

"But you saw it right there."

"I know. But I think I was breathing underwater, too, not drowning like you said."

Boppa frowned. "Breathing underwater?" Lily nodded and stared at the ground. "You don't say?" Lily nodded again without looking up. Then Boppa said, "Maybe you should tell me how you did it."

Lily's heart banged around in her chest like a bat in a box. She was determined to be understood, but when she opened her mouth, she found no words. She thought a little, mouth still open. The only explanation that came to her mind was that not knowing how she could breathe underwater was somehow connected to being able to breathe underwater. Which wasn't a very good explanation at all. Finally, defeated, she said, "I don't know what I did. I didn't do anything."

Holding a glossy green pebble up to the sun, Boppa trapped a glint of light inside of the translucent stone before putting the rock in his pocket. "Makes perfect sense to me," he replied. Lily checked his face to see if he was teasing but she couldn't say for sure. After a minute, he said, "I'll tell you what. Suppose you were breathing underwater. If that's the case, maybe we should have a signal so next time I can see that you're breathing and not drowning. Maybe stick a cattail in your hair so I know." His face was serious, and Lily's happiness filled her to the top with sparks. She adored cattails. Glancing around for his irrigation wrench, Boppa said, "We should head home."

"Are you finished irrigating?"

He shrugged. "Maybe it'll rain."

Lily was incredulous. "In July?"

"It might. It has before. Sometimes things get done when you don't do anything, remember?"

Taking a big breath, risking everything, she said, "Do you believe me?"
He paused before his reply. "I believe you believe you."

And Lily had to be satisfied. Boppa started for the pickup with long strides and Lily trotted to keep up. He looked down at her, his cowboy hat framing his face in straw. As his head tilted, a beam of sun skated a quick loop around the rim of his hat, and she had to squint one eye in the face of the glare. He said, "I was going to see if we could keep this breathing underwater to ourselves." Hoisting the irrigation wrench over his shoulder, he gave Lily a level gaze. "But I'm not sure if you're any good at keeping secrets."

"I didn't tell anybody about that time when Blaze was acting up in the corral and you threw the pitchfork at him," Lily retorted.

Her grandfather appeared mildly surprised. "Really? No one?"

"Nope."

He smiled. "Okay, then. Our secret." Lily reached up for his free hand and gave it a squeeze.

"Have I ever told you the story about the man who ran himself to death because he hated his own footprints?" Boppa asked, and this time both of them laughed because that was the whole story.

ALAN DAVIS

French Milled Soap

Carl stopped with Lucy, his daughter, after her treatment, to shop at the local mall. She was a girl who loved French milled soap. He didn't even know whether such soap was special or not. It sounded like an advertising gimmick. The first time Lucy had noticed it, in fact, had been at a Rochester hotel near the Mayo Clinic. She had been weak but had bathed for better than an hour, her sock monkey that she took everywhere staring at her with a puzzled face from its perch atop the toilet tank. Carl had called down to room service for more soap. The boy who delivered it had taken a liking to Lucy, or maybe he was just compassionate, and could tell from her shaved head – she was as bald as a baby – what the story was. He brought up a dozen soaps, each in a cardboard container with those magic words – magic for Lucy, at least – embossed in each bar in an elegant script: *French Milled Soap*.

"What exactly do the French do to soap that we don't?" he asked.

She was sweating in her robe. She gave her father an infinitely perplexed stare, as though he stood on the far side of a wide field. "It's the fragrance," she said in a tired, croaky voice. "It smells so fresh and clean."

The way she said it broke his heart. So healthy, he thought. She had her mandolin with her, standing in a corner of the room. It was an instrument the two of them had played together, but she was too weak to pick it up, much less pluck at the strings or tease out a song, and he was so tired that he could barely summon up the energy to take off his shoes and fall into bed.

It could have been any soap. "She might not live past the summer," his wife said, repeating the doc's direst prognosis, and then made a popping, puckered sound with her lips. Her tone was bitter. Lucy's life had turned to crap. And their other kid, a boy, eighteen, lived in an apartment above a bowling alley with three other kids, worked the all-night shift at a greasy spoon, and remembered maybe once a month to call. Stayed stoned all the time.

"Then again," Carl said, "the new treatment might make her better."

For her birthday, he bought her a big bag of every brand of French milled soap he could locate. It was common enough, he discovered, like French wine or French perfume. "Do the French get cancer?" he asked a clerk at a boutique.

She was a farm girl with a pageboy haircut and she stared into his gray-black beard as though he had made some weird kind of pass. "What?"

"Never mind." He lowered his head like a bull at a beauty salon. On the way home, he opened one of the bars of soap to let the fragrance fill the car. Why was it French? It wasn't made in France, but then neither was Dijon mustard. Häagen Dazs ice cream came out of The Bronx. Everything, even the latest medicine, was a marketing racket, he suspected, but that didn't make the soap, or the prescriptions, any less important.

A healer in town claimed that she could cure cancer with smells. Who knows?

He was tempted to schedule an appointment for Lucy. He believed absolutely in genetics but now knew why so many believed that somehow the soul survives the body. All this talk now about the upper world where He lived, the middle world where they lived, the lower world of vegetative beings. The idea of controlling destiny was a pleasant thought and could comfort his wife the way a stiff drink might ease the suffering of a solitary man. If a sacrifice to a local divinity like the Smell Woman would help his daughter pull through this thing, he would swerve his car to the curb, take the wood ax from its trunk, rush wild-eyed over the chain link fence, and grab the golden spaniel that was barking. He would slash its throat and sprinkle its blood over Lucy's bed as she slept, along with the vials of smells from the Smell Woman, and do the same each night, and maybe squirt whatever was left on his own wedding bed. He knew too many people, most of them his own age, who were dead or dying.

But he was not hardwired for Him.

He drove for hours and stopped twice to urinate. His cell phone was turned off. When he left the convenience store after the second stop, the day had given itself to darkness. It was a Saturday and usually he would buy a couple of lottery tickets and pick up a decent bottle of wine. It was his way of declaring that numbers could be lucky, that fate could be on his side and on the side of his family, but he had never won a thing, not even a dollar. He decided he would rather bet on Lucy's health.

The aroma of the French milled soap filled the car like a premonition and he had trouble catching his breath. He thought it might be the start of a seizure of some sort or an ocular migraine that came without warning and sometimes left him staring at matinee lights even with his eyes closed, so he pulled to the side of the road and laid back his head. His mother suffered from epilepsy and his only brother had seizures; he wondered if he had the gene and if anxiety could trigger it. When he opened his eyes, he noticed a billboard across the street, an ad for a local restaurant. "May you always have a reason to party," it read, "and someone to party with."

He repeated the jingle until he pulled into his driveway.

"Lucy," he called, feeling a panic. The house had an echo to it, as though it was still under construction. With the bag of soap in hand, he went from room to room, but couldn't find a soul.

There was a note: "Took Lucy to hospital. Where the hell are you?"

He tried his wife's cell, but it rang elsewhere in the house and he found it stuffed between the cushions on the living room couch.

A routine visit, he told himself, one I forgot about. That's what it is.

He poured a drink, a stiff one, and collapsed into a chair. He was sleepy. He wanted to sleep and to dream. Perchance to dream, he thought. Biology was no help – the vegetative beings everyone was talking about? What good did it do to think like that? And Him? He was no answer. Maybe the Smell Woman could save the day. At least she lived in the middle world with him and Lucy and everybody else.

Maybe French milled soap was a clue, the key to the labyrinth that could give them all a reason to celebrate. The fight against her cancer was like the government's battle against terror: there could be victories and defeats and you could use any weapon available, but where could you draw the line? How far were you willing to go? As far as it takes, he thought. There's the rub.

He realized that he would do anything – anything, even if it meant a trip to the ends of the earth, or down into the earth, with wads of money in his pockets – if it could cure Lucy or even keep her alive for a given amount of time.

I'd do anything, maybe even sell my soul to the devil, he decided: the chemicals the doctors administer, the new experimental therapy, the soap, the sock monkey, the Smell Woman.

He tried to pray, but to whom?

God, the universe, the technicians who administered the world, the monkey king?

He couldn't find the sock monkey. She had it with her. That was a good sign. He drifted off to sleep on the couch and dreamed that it could reach with its monkey fingers into her body as if into a steamer trunk and crush the bad cells and toss them into the air like confetti to blow away with the wind. He dreamed that Lucy was building, with the help of invisible creatures, an indestructible fortress, one composed of thousands of bricks of French milled soap.

For more work from Alan Davis, look for his short story collection *So Bravely Vegetative* from Hollywood Books International.

ROGER REAL DROUIN

Gray

Under the clouds like gray plates crashing into each other. Here he was, chasing true scientific endeavor.

The photographer of birds hiked further into the 26,000-acre South Carolina pine bluff, the wind heavy with that wet coldness. The rain would be coming soon.

He knew he was chasing a ghost.

He hiked further along the two-rutted park service trail. The rain would come within the hour, he thought, but despite the pale white-gray sky, it felt good to be in the field again. The strong coffee in his thermos and the new snug-fitting hiking boots were the two modest but reassuring checks in the positive column. From the boots to the cotton-canvas pants and the thick flannel and heavy rucksack, the photographer was prepared for the weather, and the movement of the hike kept him warm.

He was searching for the Northern Stilted Curlew, one of the world's rarest birds, a species last documented in 1961. This arctic shorebird was what is called a grail bird – it may or may not exist. In Samuel's big four-volume *Master Guide to Birding*, the Curlew was listed as "probably extinct." A color sketch showed the sturdy, dull-looking bird capable of flying the longest annual migration of any species, other than a handful of sea birds that can stop and rest on the water. Every September, the Curlew fattens up on crowberries, worms, and insect larvae, before flying south to the end of the continent, logging in close to 10,000 miles on the flyway.

Just about every ornithologist and biologist in the world favored the more unfortunate outcome: the last Northern Stilted Curlew had decades ago made its last annual migration north to south.

Samuel heard the pines crush before he saw the two figures ambling towards him. He expected to see more birders along the trail, at least a few of those semi-retired, Tilley-hat-wearing folks who check the rare birds database on the web nightly. But the weather had kept them home.

Or maybe, most just reasoned it was not worth the trip. A less rare, but much more plausible sighting, such as the Kirtland's Warbler, or an accidental sighting of a species way out of its range, like the Cuban PeWee in South Florida, would draw dozens in pursuit.

Here in these pines forty hours earlier, an amateur had spotted what he *thought* was the Northern Stilted Curlew. This same scenario happens often.

An excited birder could easily mistake the long bill, dark brow marking, and the strong, rapid wing beats of the white-bellied, stilted Whimbrel for that of the Curlew. From a distance, it's also easy to confuse the long stilted legs of the Northern Stilted Curlew to those of the Stilted Sandpiper. The Curlew's delicate pinkish buff under the wing, the decurved bill, and its unique call would be the most distinguishing features.

"See anything?" he asked the couple.

"Nothing but a bunch of squirrels," the wife said.

The man wore long pants and a Columbia rain slicker over layers, a hunting style-cap, and a small hiking pack. The woman wore the standard, floppy Tilley hat and shorts with long socks. She had a fleece on, and binoculars, and a Canon SLR around her neck.

"And a few Carolina Wrens and one Ruffled Titmouse," the husband added. "It's been pretty quiet."

"They'll be out when the rain clears," Samuel said.

"If it clears," the man said.

They knew he was here for the Curlew.

"We drove up from Fort Lauderdale," the woman said. They were die-hards, Samuel thought. "She was seen near here, not far, right?"

The sex of the possibly-observed curlew in question had been unknown. If it was in fact a Curlew, it would be difficult to distinguish the sex – both sexes look very similar, only the female is slightly smaller, and an immature can be mistaken for a female. It would be very difficult to determine if it were a female, unless the bird was seen up close. Samuel had written down the notification from the online Rare Bird Database: *Reported Northern Stilted Curlew...unconfirmed sighting...sighted at Darney Bluff National Preserve...four and a half miles northeast of the main trailhead...directly north of the old hunting check-in station along a short loop trail...the bird was observed for thirty seconds before it alighted and flew in a north-north east direction.*

"The report said four and a half miles northeast of the main trailhead, directly north of the old hunting check-in station, which is about a mile further," Samuel said.

"We were out that far, near the check-in station," the husband said and looked up. "That thunder doesn't sound good."

So they were there, Samuel thought. That doesn't matter. If the Curlew was still in this pine bluff, she could be in the same area, but not the same exact location. After the rain, she would fly east towards the marsh and eventually back out over the Atlantic. She was more than halfway to her wintering destination, and she wouldn't wait behind here.

Scientists consider sightings of extremely rare species to be only hypotheses that require rigorous examination. A bird presumed by many to be extinct would meet with disbelief, and scorn. For Samuel, a peculiar observation in the Everglades four years ago, combined with a list of other reports, formed his hypothesis that the species was not extinct. There's a lot of space left from northern Canada to Argentina for a handful of birds to become nearly invisible.

Only true scientific endeavor could reject or accept his hypothesis.

He kneeled in the dark space, took the small tarp from his rucksack, and folded it atop the layer of pine needles. He tilted the mug, sipping the last of the coffee, including the crunchy grind sediment the filter didn't catch. Some of it stays on his tongue, grainy and bitter, before he swallows it down. He put the empty thermos into one of the compartments. He took out the 200mm lens and clicked it onto his favorite camera, an older digital Nikon. The Nikon was a few inches bigger and heavier than the newer models, and Samuel liked the sturdiness of it. He set the 300mm lens on top of the pack where he could reach it. The two plates of egg-and-bacon he had at the hotel would be wearing off soon. He took out two of the granola bars from the side compartment.

Waiting it out, leaning against the back of the old three-walled hunting station, he was grateful for the half-rotten, paint-long-gone structure that stood between him and the *ptttt plunk plunk* of the rain beginning to fall on the rusted roof.

He leaned back against the shelter, his arms around his knees so only a few drops of the rain slanting down into the black soil splashed onto his boots. The wind came though in an unsteady whistle. It was high-pitched, silencing all other sounds, and then hesitant but rhythmic. Without the motion of the hike to keep him warm, the photographer of birds rubbed his hands together.

His country was being torn apart, and the divide was growing. Out here, he ate the granola bar and sipped some water, and listened to the wind. Out here, he felt right, cold but dry and sure that he was where he was supposed to be.

He hadn't questioned it, the reasoning for being out in the field looking for the Northern Stilted Curlew, and he wouldn't let the doubt start now. There were many things he had second-guessed – he had once considered faith. He thought of everything he really had faith in. He had forty-six years to think about religion, and he was still formulating his take on it, but he did have faith in God's judgment over man. And a judgment would come.

He had faith in dreams, dreams that sank right down into the images and sounds of thought. He had faith in the memories of his dreams.

The memory of his wife when she was disappearing in the hospital, and how she would smile in the middle of the pain when he walked in. That was some kind of faith she had. A friend had told him once that he could move on, try to meet someone new. His friend was only trying to help.

Samuel thought about his son, how when he was just a boy, four or five, all he'd want to do is hide up in his closet and sketch giraffes.

"It isn't hiding," Lorine had said to Samuel. "The boy is living. Look at how happy he is."

Samuel worried because his son could remove himself from the world the way his father could. Lorine would tell him it was OK, their son was a beautiful, extraordinary boy, he was thoughtful and liked to draw, and if that meant he was a little different, who cares if he would rather spend the day sitting by a lamp in his closet sketching while every other boy on the street rode their bicycles in a pack?

She loved Ry so much, and maybe she loved him more because the boy had this different look in his eyes, eyes deep green like the different shades of a forest mixed all together. She loved the boy fiercely. She kept him grounded, but through her respect for him, she also kept him from changing. Even before he could walk, she idolized him. It was her idea to encourage him to apply to the new arts charter high school and the scholarship to college. The boy was always thinking of his drawings, and in many ways he was just like his old man, but Samuel worried because he knew it would easier for the boy to imagine less and interact more.

And now, thirteen months after his wife's death, Samuel saw how his son was walking the way a young man would when he was detaching himself further from the world. He was walking like no one could see him. Samuel hoped that his son could stand it, at least get through all the scary parts.

He looked out, through the rain.

Once the clouds cleared, the pines would let squares of sunlight flow through. But now it was a shade between blue and gray under the pines. The high-pitched *hak hak hak hak* came above the wind, from the east. He leaned outside the shelter to hear the Peregrine Falcon's coming from the top branches of a Maple tree about three hundred yards off. Placing the camera and tripod on the pine needles and adjusting the aperture to let more light in the lens, through the viewfinder it appeared – the bluish brown feathers and the dark gray malar stripe, and the broad wings tucked along his side. He snapped a dozen photos, with the falcon looking down, towards the shelter, and sharply at the man with the camera before ascending at an angle a jet could never pull off.

He viewed the photos on the Nikon's screen, and zoomed in on the one gray and blue falcon that came out in perfect focus. In the winter of '95, across an open prairie in Superior, Wisconsin, he watched a Peregrine, only slightly larger than this one, pursue and strike a Ring-necked Pheasant. The speed and power of that bird was truly remarkable. Pheasant feathers exploded from that bird when it was struck. It was one of the photos he was most proud of.

The rain had stopped, as he knew it would, but the gray lingered. There would be no sun this afternoon. He packed up the rucksack, leaving out the camera, which he slung across his neck.

He hiked north on the park service trail, past the Maple the falcon had flown from. He looked up and stopped every few yards to listen. It was his habit. His son said he always had his head in the clouds. He turned down the narrow single track east now. After a half-mile, he heard another call. But this stopped him in his tracks. It was a call he'd never heard before, a call from a bird in flight that he could not locate.

Samuel stopped and listened. He had been walking when he heard it, and he knew sounds heard while walking could be distorted. Please, let me hear it again, he thought. Please, fly this way. The only movement he made was inching his fingers to the Nikon, to feel that it was there. It was a sound that matched descriptions he had read, a sound that no one had ever recorded.
He did not hear the sound again. He listened, standing then sitting under the wrinkled trunk of a tall pine, looking up into the sky. He took his field journal and pen from his rucksack. With the journal to a new, unmarked page, he wrote his location as best as he could describe it, noting how far he was down the trail past the narrow creek bed and describing the pine taller than the other trees.

When he got to writing the sound, he found there was no exact language to describe it. It was a soft whistle – no not a whistle – that was the word that had been imparted in his memory from reported accounts of the Northern Stilted Curlew. In 1949, after the species was already decimated from intense hunting and disappearing habitat, Frank Kerrson saw a pair of Northern Stilted Curlews, and described their call as "a low tremulous whistle." Audubon, who had painted the Curlew for his *Birds of America*, described the call as a soft whistle.

Samuel scribbled and crossed out and then wrote: *It was like someone trying to whistle loudly but blowing air. Like that, but more musical. The bird called in series of threes in the same pitch, not more than three series, before all sound broke off as quickly as it came. I stopped in time to hear, without the distortion of movement, the last series of faint calls tee-teeee-teeee.*

He listened, looking up to the rain falling again, the gray lacking light. He listened for the bird to call one more time. An hour later, he headed back towards the trailhead, still listening.

Rain dripping off his hat low, he walked past the perfectly still fox looking out from his den of green. The man's boot steps were the only sound beside the rain falling on the pines.

KATHERINE L. HOLMES

An Elderly Woman and an Adolescent

"Is the girl upstairs yours?"

The customer was hesitating from writing "Victorian House Antiques" in her checkbook. Lloyd had prepared Lil Butterstead for the banter that led to last-minute dickerings about price. Opals jiggled from the woman's ears and a gold bracelet girded her Bulova watch.

"A girl? They often stray from their mothers. Was she in the room with the doll schoolhouse or the room with the cradle?" Mrs. Butterstead humored the woman's reluctance to write a three-figure amount for an inlaid table. People had excused themselves from buying it after they saw the pegs for spools of thread in the table's drawer.

"She's wearing cut-off jeans with lace at the hem. They almost looked like bloomers," the woman dawdled.

"Hmmmm." Mrs. Butterstead noticed a girl who was familiar to her in a disturbing way. "The table, as I told you, was custom-made. People are so drawn to the mother-of-pearl inlay. You could easily have the pegs in the drawer sawed off. A little sanding and it's just for you." Lloyd would have detested such a suggestion. "A driver's license should be sufficient. My partners will be back from Chicago Monday if you need our help lifting it."

"That won't be necessary. My husband is over there. I guess he wants to buy some marbles."

He was solid as a cast iron safe. Her eyesight worsening because of diabetes, Mrs. Butterstead couldn't make Braille of the woman's embossed license number.

"I'm losing my marbles," Mrs. Butterstead said, ringing up the sum. "My husband knew where to get those marbles, the old milk glass ones," she explained. "He passed on this year and so did my marbles chum from childhood. But I can hold the door for you."

The gall of the woman, Mrs. Butterstead mused with a smile stuck on her face as the couple conveyed the table past the oak door. To insinuate that she would post a girl in the upstairs bedroom wearing something flimsy and resembling Victorian underwear! But this was the weekend when thefts might surpass the pay of a shop assistant.

If Adele, her marbles chum, had seen the stairwell wallpaper with the bleeding hearts, she would have been reminded of the back staircases of her childhood home. The banker's house.

But Adele's obituary was in the metro newspaper two months after her husband died. Because Lil Butterstead was following the traffic signals of her circulation now, she paused on the staircase to straighten a photograph. It was a prairie-scape like the environs of her hometown. And during the Depression, all cloud and loam. That was when Lloyd began creeping up the banker's back stairs like a cat burglar. Skillful pool player that he was, he had shown her how to set up mirrors in the turret area of the Victorian antique house.

From the turret, Mrs. Butterstead could already view the girl in the nice bedroom as she talked about the mirrors with a customer.

"The design on the border of this mirror makes me think of the temple-style banks they built early in the century. Before the Crash, of course. Yes, that's a lovely Maxfield Parrish print in the rustic bedroom."

After garden parties at the banker's house, Lil and Adele used to loll about on the lawn, their lemonade glasses on silver coasters.

"Oh yes, this commercial mirror would be wonderful for a lake place. Or a lodge. With the girl fishing out of it." But Mrs. Butterstead was watching the girl with the lace strips cross the hall from the nice bedroom and wander into the rustic bedroom.

Herding the customer into the rustic bedroom, Mrs. Butterstead let her examine the Maxfield Parrish print while she sidled near the girl. An heirloom embroidered teapot warmer had tempted the girl to look at the pricetag. Meanwhile, the customer postponed buying the Parrish print. Mrs. Butterstead assured her that husbands needed to be consulted.

"Are you looking for a gift?" she asked the girl.

There had to be many girls similar to this one: hair the gleaming brown of tea, its ends a crochet of curl; tea-colored eyes behind glasses; around a hundred pounds, maybe five feet, three inches; about fourteen years old. That would have been Adele's statistics then. Yet Mrs. Butterstead had forgotten the exact features of her face. All the metro obit told was Adele's age and the names of her survivors, her husband and five children.

The girl nodded and continued looking through the linens.

A woman in a tulip-red blouse had come in. "Since you're up here, could I get you to open this cabinet case? I'm wondering about this plate."

Mrs. Butterstead did have Braille for the keys in her pocket. "That's a series of plates called 'Life on the Western Prairies.' Royal Cornwall and very reasonable."

The girl had her back to Mrs. Butterstead and she was working her way around to the applewood bookcase. She took out one of Mrs. Butterstead's favorites, a book on Buckingham Palace.

Mrs. Butterstead gabbed, "It's funny to think that when people began settling here, a boy named Tom Cotton was found in Queen Victoria's palace. He had hidden himself in her chimneys. He lived there a year, which explained some sooty sheets. Better to earn passage to American then, huh?"

The girl put the book back and like a piece of furniture on wheels, she slid around the room until Mrs. Butterstead was watching her in the fishpond mirror, descending the stairs.

"It is amazing, isn't it? That boy in Buckingham Palace. There were only a few items missing. Two inkstands, a sword, and a pair of trousers."

That afternoon, a thirteen-year-old girl named Lorna Samuelson was reading an article on family violence in the newspaper. *Children who watch violence are more likely to resort to it themselves,* she pondered as her father wrenched the front door open. His mood that week made him remote yet firm about rituals. He didn't need to repeat his request for Lorna to surrender the newspaper.

Lorna-just-like-her-father.

She watched her father skip over the home section, hurdle to the sports pages, and then return to the front page, what he did every day. Then he put down the newspaper and went to get a beer, daring anyone to take the newspaper from his chair.

Lorna didn't believe she was so dumb as monkey-see, monkey-do. She couldn't imagine herself doing what her parents did last year before vacation. They were going on vacation tomorrow morning and the argument had already started last night.

Lorna, her brother Skip, and her little sister Kelsey had eaten early, at 4:30, so her mother could clean out the refrigerator and get them ready for traveling. Her father had gotten off at 3:00, but he came home later than he'd promised. The early dinner pork chops, done in brown sugar sauce, were tarry when they were reheated. They stuck to her father's teeth, he complained.

He had run into his old friend Rando. "That's right, Randy. He's the one who could afford an architect to plan his log lake cabin." They could spend a few days there or at a campsite nearby if they all liked camping so much.

"You had hard liquor during your happy hour," Lorna's mother remarked. "Listen. We've got to move your mother's furniture to the basement. You said you'd have that done yesterday."

"You've varnished the pork chops," Lorna's father said.

They were eating early, Lorna's mother reminded him.

He thought she had her furniture refinishing class that day. She could hardly stand to miss it during vacation. It wasn't every day that he ran into Rando and today was happy hour.

That was the trouble with him. He might have called. But she supposed that he was acting like the Jolly Green Outdoors Guy again. If he was going to start behaving like someone who had never known a home like his mother's... Lorna's mother didn't say what she would do but her voice had some finish to it.
Home! If she would think of him for once! He wanted that walnut furniture sold right from the garage. She cooked for the children and planned her meals around her classes. Candied pork chops! Lucky her, he could eat camping provisions. She might have told him that she lived on salads before they got married.

Instead of packing up in her room, Lorna sat in the living room with Skip, playing Chinese checkers. From there, she could see the pork chop plummeting to the linoleum. At least it wasn't a china plate. Their retriever, Zappa, played hockey with it, enraging her mother.

As if he thought of her! Now she had to scrub the floor again! They'd come back to ants or worse!

Lorna's five-year-old sister Kelsey screamed. She wanted a marble but Skip held it tightly, his head turned towards the kitchen.

Now he had upset the children, Lorna's mother cried, coming into the living room to comfort Kelsey.

Lorna's father followed her. *The walnut furniture would make their living room look like a modular morgue.*

As if his mother's chairs would make him mournful, not the money that wasn't so solid. He shouldn't be using her as an excuse to act sick. This manic-macho stuff. Happy with Randy and who could like his downside at home?

Did he care? Lorna's father's hand rested on the glass plant stand. He had to demonstrate how the copper girders wobbled at its base, making its three round wedding cake tiers unsteady.

Lorna and Skip cleared out of the way. Kelsey crawled into the cubby of the living room desk. Lorna ran upstairs and got her new lavender tape deck from her room. She sat on the stairs, playing Blood and Roses at low volume, risking her father hearing it. He'd probably rail about the tape deck and throw it like the pork chop, calling it or the music junk. If tonight was like last year, he would be easier on her than her mother.

She couldn't sell the rattan furniture that had gotten them into debt! If it was time for new furniture, she made a mistake.
Lorna could see her father kicking at the couch leg to make his point. Then he fell back on the plant stand. Its glass disks toppled along with cascading baby's tears, hoya rope, and jade figurines. It all broke over the fireplace brick, the impact mixing with wails.

"Oh, you didn't want to move that?" Lorna's father wheedled in his alcohol voice. He swore about a marble being underfoot.

Lorna listened for the crunch of the refrigerator door and the wheeze of the screen door. Then she heard her mother on the telephone. She ran into the living room and stooped over the torrent of roots and leaves. Then she got the fireside broom and started sweeping the dirt towards the grate, only to find that the jade deer had lost an antler. Behind her, Skip picked up blunt pieces of glass.

"Get *away* from that glass. Has it cut your hand?" Lorna's mother was sitting near Kelsey, examining her with one hand on the phone. *No, they were all right and could come in the car. It was parked out front since they had furniture in their garage. He might have injured the youngest. Glass flying around. She wasn't sure. He would have liked to do that to her, yes, he wanted to hurt her.*

Lorna and Skip had to go upstairs and pack, she said.

At the landing window, Lorna saw her father at the backyard grill, already shaping a hamburger for it. She raced her mother, stuffing basics and visitor's clothing into her canvas camping satchel. With her woods tread, she decided to avoid the women's shelter. A motley group of women were always sitting on the porch there, not caring who saw them from the street. That's what her father said when they drove past.

Lorna was already downstairs when her mother came from Skip's bedroom on the first floor. As soon as her mother went upstairs, Lorna called, "I'm going to Brenda's house."

She was at the front door when she heard her mother call "Lorna!", not catching up with her, not stopping her. Sprinting away, Lorna took the avenue. Then she ran through the alleyways until she was across from Victorian House Antiques. She passed the benches with carved-out hearts and went in under the stained glass lintel.

"As I said, these are all Royal Cornwall 'Life on the Western Prairies' plates. The top one makes me think of Michelangelo – the boy and girl trying to touch hands as they ride horses. Something like that happened when I was a girl only the boy was on snowshoes and I wasn't so I sank. These plates can go separately."

Since Lloyd was gone, so many objects tempted Mrs.

Butterstead with memories. What the plate evoked would not melt from her mind if she got as brittle as an icicle. As Mrs. Butterstead waited for the woman, gesturing for her friend now, she browsed the bedroom for shoplifted items.

Adele was a girl she could never catch up with, a girl in a white rabbit hood and trimmings.

She kept thinking that Adele's coat was white too, people wore so much white then. But it was Adele who wore the snowshoes that Lloyd carved and wove with rawhide.

Lloyd promised that the banker's daughter would walk on waves after a blizzard.

The scene seemed so bridal, Adele with her hands in a rabbit muff and the snowshoes lagging behind her like a train. Beforehand, Lloyd led Lil to the drifts, demonstrating to Adele's father how Lil became mired in the snow while he and his snowshoes stayed atop it. The banker peered at her, his sight much poorer than he knew, and then he paid Lloyd the precious few dollars for Adele's snowshoes.

Lloyd and Adele surmounted the banks of the stream on their snowshoes and then they tumbled onto the ice, sliding down the wide, sinuous aisle.

Mrs. Butterstead watched the two women knelling like bells over the Royal Cornwall plates. They both wore silk blouses and sported pointy haircuts. Gratified, she allowed a few minutes for an attachment. "I'll be in the hallway," she said.

In the banker's house, the scrolled mahogany cabinets with their bear-like bases awed Lloyd out of self-consciousness. Adele's mother set out two more lunch plates of Spode when the snowshoes were a success. Lil had been going over to Adele's to listen to the phonograph. She and Lloyd were like two waifs in

Queen Victoria's sloppy palace. But it was only a banker's house with back stairways.

Lil checked the nicer bedroom where the doll schoolhouse was set up. Most girls that age were fascinated with its thimble-sized bell and the marble-sized globe on the teacher's desk. Adele would have wanted it even though she had a fourteen-room doll's house. No, everything was there and on the white-painted vanity that her partners found. The crystal perfume bottles, the bead purse.

She felt uneasy lately with the things that had outlasted people. Especially those that reminded her of a day when the snow sparkled like Fostoria. She and Adele talking in Adele's bedroom about going to college and having splendid weddings. It all crashed so quickly.

"How are you with the plates?" Mrs. Butterstead asked the ladies in daffodil and tulip silk. "My husband would have liked them. He was quite a history buff. After the Depression, people couldn't afford college so easily. I'm still not clear about how President Reagan went."

"His ambiance makes him more appreciated," said the lady in daffodil. "I like this plate with the children on horses so much better than the others. But one plate seems so out-of-context."

"It's Cornwall's combination of Laura Ingalls Wilder and Michelangelo," Lil said.

"We'll be back," said the woman in the tulip silk. "If she wants it at home, she'll be back tomorrow."

The sale of the snowshoes started the afternoons at Adele's, Mrs. Butterstead reminisced to herself as she opened a jewelry case for two college kids. The girl had to handle an antique enamel chatelaine.

The banker didn't know they were in his house unless she and Lloyd laughed on the back staircase. They could smell his cigar trail. Lloyd had been studying the phonograph cabinet in the study. And then he took an ax to the cabinet he was building, reducing it to firewood. He had to saw down trees for fuel, out in the woods earning hardly anything.

"Yes, there's time for you to see the upstairs before we close," Mrs. Butterstead said to the young couple. And she wanted to make sure that the candleholders were still in the bedrooms, Candlewick and the floral porcelain ones.

Since Lloyd was gone, Mrs. Butterstead liked closing up at the Victorian house. Tonight though, the used canopy bed frame upstairs bothered her. A jolt when her partners brought it in. She should remember such a bed as the perch of two Maxfield Parrish girls.

Lil and Adele giggling about bundling. That was a country custom of some German farm neighbors, the rumor went around the high school. The young man climbed into his fiance's bedroom to bundle, occupying her bed for a few hours. Adele had wondered, "Do you believe they kept their clothes on?" Lil sang a song because she didn't know how to answer her. Lil's parents said that only people in a sect bundled and people in sects had schisms.

But then one late afternoon, Lil walked in on Lloyd and Adele. Lloyd was leaving town the next day.

The Candlewick candleholders were still there.

But the canopy bed – there was a nude shoulder and Adele's silk slip on the floor. She stared at Lloyd under the counterpane, and at his bare foot beyond the edge of it. Lil sank downstairs, feeling much worse than she did when they were on snowshoes and she wasn't.

The young man's smile was discreet as he pointed out a vintage seed pearl necklace downstairs. He left his girlfriend in the antique house kitchen while he bought it.

Lloyd looked that way when Lil complained about their daughter co-habitating with her boyfriend. It was just as well that he kept sleeping with her, Lloyd argued. As usual, he was right. Ruth Ann wanted some old garters and an old cameo brooch for her wedding.

Locking up, Mrs. Butterstead still had a forboding that someone had gone over her head in the painted lady house. She hadn't followed the girl downstairs, she thought as she examined the costume jewelry and the glass. The animal-covered milk glass dishes, dolphin and cat and squirrel, looked undisturbed. And the Hummel figurines.

Her partners would notice if anything were missing. If they thought Lil couldn't handle the store anymore, they would capitulate and hire a shop assistant. She was capable enough when Lloyd was alive. Her partners usually splurged at the Chicago antique show, bringing back odds and ends that required Lloyd's advice. She was still useful when it came to the wayward pieces of Depression glass.

From under a table of linens, Lorna heard the old woman humming and then muttering something about Adele.

"Adele knew the words. They had the phonograph."

The old woman thought she was alone. She didn't know that Lorna had loitered in the kitchen of the Victorian house, pretending to be interested in jugs that she might play in a band. When she heard the old cash register dinging at closing time, she eluded the old lady, slipped upstairs, and crawled under the table. If the old lady found her, she had some handkerchiefs that she could say dropped down. The tablecloth didn't quite hang to the floor, but Lorna crouched against the wall.

She thought she might start sobbing when she saw the old woman's foam-heeled shoes doddering as if her feet were asleep. The old woman resembled a silver sugar bowl. Lorna couldn't imagine her doing anything without discussion.

There used to be an old man here, her husband. His hair was like pigeon feathers and he was as dignified as an old clock when he gave Lorna twists of hard candy, stopping her from petting china Chihuahuas. Lorna's mother brought the old man a bureau drawer that had become unhinged and then a chair that needed its seat rewoven. A few weeks ago, Lorna's mother talked the blue streak of a Friday afternoon with the old woman about the walnut furniture while Lorna wandered around the store.

When dusk shadows trudged the floor like watchmen, Lorna sat on the floor near the table, staring at objects that reminded her of her grandparents' house. The plate with a girl and a boy on horseback almost touching hands. A huge, hammer-armed chair that was all buttoned around. An old pitcher and jug like the one Lorna's grandmother got out when Lorna had a fever at her house. The framed old photograph of a woman wearing black. Porcelain doorknobs.

Since she had scared herself motionless under the table, Lorna felt as glum as the face in the old photograph. The woman seemed severe, staring at the beautiful picture of two girls sitting near some columns.

Lorna had whiled away the evening reading the book on Buckingham Palace. She'd found the part about a boy hiding there. And now she shivered as all the comforting objects disappeared into the dark. She might as well have gone to the women's shelter.

It happens about twice a year, she would be telling someone. *After Christmas and before we go on vacation and then sometimes in between. My dad gets drunk and starts picking out some object to bash up. He usually says it's because my mother* made a poor purchase. But I think she sold my grandmother's plates because of him doing that. I guess he went to parties called bashes before I was born. His hair was long then. He broke a pottery vase because he said the cave drawings on it weren't any good. He dented a no-stick pan. Last summer, he threw beer on some new drapes that my mother chose. It's scary and I usually run from the room. But so far he's like a fender bender and nobody gets hurt. He doesn't have fender benders; my mother does.

Lorna is in the dark, her mother would say. *Look at her, playing vampire. He hasn't laid a hand on her.*

The women at the shelter would probably know that policemen had visited their house. When they warned her father, he swaggered back at them and said things like, "What I give in this house I can take away."

The unpredictable snoring sounds from the road kept Lorna going over and over what she knew. Even though she didn't want to go to the women's shelter, she might have to tomorrow.

My mother is always exaggerating, she might blurt out. *My father says she exaggerates every time she goes shopping. And then last summer, after the drapes, they were so lovey-dovey on vacation. Now my mom's gone back to school and my dad is mad because there's not as much money.*

I think my father treats my mother worse than he treats anyone. In our neighborhood, everyone says hi to him since he went around demonstrating how to recycle. He even gave a bash and showed people how to stomp on cans.

Somewhere downstairs, a clock called out the cusp of her usual night: cuckoo, cuckoo, cuckoo. Ten times. A nice dad turning villain. Though Lorna, being a camper, had more tolerance for unyielding surfaces than most girls, she became the bump in the night. Towards the kerosene glow of a streetlight, she budged along the floor on a small braid rug, staying near the bookcase. An old cradle was near the cabinet with the plates. But then she saw her own silhouette, what wasn't supposed to be there, in a hall mirror.

Lorna sat near the hall, looking at the room that was now in black and ghost. It reminded her of her grandmother's wake, all the old people on the walnut furniture. Lorna suddenly understood how guilt made people afraid of ghosts. Ghosts were from a time that was more prim, a time when people wore twilight clothing and grim expressions in photographs. She wouldn't like to know their opinions.

The shadows fluttered over the linens like fingers. *She didn't have to marry him! Look what's happened of her own free will. Ha!*

And that young body isn't being made to mind anyone, the darkness on a bentwood rocker would probably answer like an old woman at the wake. *It's true, there were bruises on my arm under the long sleeve. As if the men out here were all gentlemen!*

Stolidly the hammer-armed chair loomed out. *I sat across from a television and watched what all our work was for. Enough to tempt the bark off an oak tree. And then they get into a temper because it's all tantalizing.*

Lorna wanted to run howling down to the veranda of the Victorian house and along the street. But she was locked inside Victorian House Antiques and like a ghost, she had to avoid physical contact with anything solid. Unless she lit the candle on the bookshelf. Then she might see the picture of the two girls and the heavenly sky above them. Riffling in her satchel for matches, Lorna couldn't remember whether the wick on the candle was white or sooty.

The candle flame intensified the streetlight glow. She impetuously put it out. Then she saw that the clouds were threadbare outside and the moon was shining through the partially drawn lace curtains. The room seemed to have developed into shades of old photographs. Lorna felt more calm, as if she were looking at lens calibrations when the eye doctor switched them and asked: "Better or worse?"

But out in the hall, she discerned what looked like a ghost, the ghost of the Victorian house. Nodding in silver and alabaster, it was coming from the room with the canopy bed and the doll schoolhouse. Holding her scream, Lorna saw that the ghost was like starlight. But the mirrors in the hallway were reflecting moonlight back and forth. There was a breeze and trees outside the windows, shifting the light. She looked from one mirror to the other, the girl fishing into the eerie light. She was the ghost, watching for another ghost until she was dreaming it. The hallway was a wishing well and words were being tossed into it.

Better or worse? Worse or better? Does she think it will get better or worse? Is it better to stay around for the worse? Or is it worse to expect better? Did she think she could help his worse get better? How much worse is her better getting? Who is getting the better of whom? If they get through lots of worse, can they expect better-than-ever? Who is whose better? Should they have said at first, "Has it ever been better? How worse can your worse get?" When they've never felt better, they can say they'll take the worse. Maybe it's better that way. Or was it worse?

The sunlight made its return with its strong statements, that it was the moonlight, the starlight, the real thing and better, the unreal dawn. And that this day would be better. In the morning wakefulness that insomniacs know, Lorna told herself that she would not spend another sleepless night in Victorian House Antiques. Pulling shafts of her hair into a barrette, looking into a mirror with roses and ribbons on its perimeters, Lorna could see another side of herself with her better eye.

She changed clothes, putting on what runaways are not often

described as wearing – a summer shift. Made of liver-spotted cream cotton, it had a dropped waist and one casual ruffle. Considering a chamber pot, Lorna had to keep moving, dancing and driven as a sprite, until she found a blocked-off bathroom.

After the rooster-loud cash register became activated and Lorna heard a carousel of creaking, she emerged from under the linen table, feeling like a breathing object.

"There was a time a person could be a butterfingers with these glasses," Mrs. Butterstead commented as a girl in her twenties bought wineglasses with the name "Dionysus" on them. But she said it to another customer, one she meant to help with Depression glass. The younger woman, her purse a rumple of hemp, was in a hurry to have the Dionysus glasses. Mrs. Butterstead wrapped them as skimpily as the girl was dressed.

She furnished a history of the glasses. "My husband knew the proprietors of Dionysus so when the restaurant closed, they called me about their glassware. Collector's items for anyone in this area. But you know, they got these glasses for the breaking. Years ago, when they did as the Greeks did at Dionysus, my husband threw his wine glass at the hearth. He said it had a releasing effect. I couldn't do it."

Mrs. Butterstead was relieved that the young woman went away without socializing, her bracelets clanking as if they were made from an alloy of tin cans.

The woman who was asking about the Depression glass paused between the parlor and the dining room, looking upstairs as if she were assessing a rain cloud. "Is the girl upstairs yours?"

"What girl? No. She must be with a customer." Mrs. Butterstead hadn't seen a girl come in. But there was a starburst effect when the front door opened to the morning sun.

"She was standing at the case with the plates. I asked her about them," the woman said, heading towards the Depression glass in the parlor.

Watching the staircase from the parlor, Mrs. Butterstead said, "We were lucky to get plates with that celery dish and platter. It's called Mayfair and it came out in 1933, I think. They're expensive but there's not much Depression glass in blue, you know."

Pneumonia blue, Lil thought. *At home, Lil ate on pink Depression glass. Adele had stopped eating in 1938, just after her father immured himself at his bank. And her mother, always wearing that fawn silk, gave a disgruntled former garden party guest a choice between their Spode china and their silver tea service. It was only a few months after Lloyd left. Adele's skin had the sheen of a fever and when Lloyd visited her in the spring, her body was blue and bosomless under the canopy of her bed.*
"Yes, the blue is so delicate. It makes a lovely table display," the customer said.

That was the last time Lloyd saw Adele.

The Mayfair plates were vein blue, the color Mrs. Butterstead looked for when she gave herself insulin shots. Plump after her pregnancy in 1946, she found out she had diabetes. Whenever Lil gained weight, she had to go back on the insulin. Lloyd handled her like Depression glass, put her on a shelf. He hated things that were tawdry, hated thinking about needles, made such a point of his own health, talking about the furniture he had to move when he dropped her off at the hospital. She knew at those times, when he hardly touched her, thoughtful as he was, he had deserted Adele.

"I can't promise any more of the Mayfair. But we might be getting more Depression glass in – pink and called Poppy. One of my partners has it stored. But you can't count on any pieces. They get separated from their sets, the way people did during the Depression. I had a friend who was well off one year, ill from malnutrition the next, and the next year, she had gone away to clean rooms in a boarding house that her relatives made of their home. If you need me, I'll be upstairs for a few minutes."

That was what it was about then, the lugging of a spiritless leg up the stairs when there didn't seem to be much point to it.

Lil avoided Adele too. There was that taint of retribution everywhere, and she was tending the vegetable garden that her parents made of their front lawn. People made jokes about Adele reading in her canopy bed when she couldn't go to college. Lil had to wonder if Jeanne spilled what Lil told her about Adele and Lloyd – Jeanne seemed so sensible. Adele wrote Lil postcards from the city, from the house of her poorer relations. "It's embarrassing. The people with eastern accents pronounce it 'bawding house.'"

The last time Lil wrote Adele, all she said was that the cabbages had a blight and she wouldn't grow them again.

Resting herself at the landing, Mrs. Butterstead looked for a girl's reflection in the hallway mirrors. Which bedroom was she in?

After Adele's last letter, she examined herself in her bedroom mirror. Adele had protested in her spired hand, "They made me marry." At nineteen, Lil could estimate the angle of Lloyd's rebound when he found out. And her compensation for showing Lloyd the words on the next page: "He has a job. He's very smart with automobiles. He can maintain them."

Mrs. Butterstead's face was still full and creamy, its wrinkles only hairline, like a cup of Spode. She couldn't help but notice as she looked for the girl in the mirrors and the doorways. In the rustic bedroom, the braid rug had pulled near the hall. It looked awful near the bleeding hearts wallpaper.

If a girl was upstairs alone, she was unusual not to have moved the tiny books and the dolls in the doll schoolhouse. Children wanted to shake the miniature bell and it had a tinny ding. But there wasn't a girl in the bedroom with the canopy bed.

There was only Lloyd's ax splitting a porch bench like the miniature benches in the schoolhouse, and his anger after he accused the banker of bartering his daughter. Lil married Lloyd anyway. The wedding was as pristine as Haviland china when there was only Depression glass for the reception.

But there was that girl now, looking like Adele in a low-waisted dress after the world had changed and Lloyd had sympathized about Ruth Ann's co-habitating with her boyfriend. The girl was looking piqued near the antique cradle.

Yes, Lil wanted everything that girl might have had then.

Mrs. Butterstead wandered around, straightening the linens. Then she was piqued, seeing a candle that had been lit and put out. They sold their candleholders with new candles in them.

"Just think, that cradle is probably from the Victorian period," Mrs. Butterstead said to the girl, the girl from last night, she was sure now. A familiar girl with those intent tea-colored eyes and hair like swirled tea on a sunny day.

"Of course the cradle is a Midwestern piece. A primitive, we call them in the antique business."

The girl peered at her through her glasses.

"Just think of it," Mrs. Butterstead said, relating her favorite story from Lloyd's history reading. "When Queen Victoria was reigning in England, there were two boys who hid themselves in Buckingham Palace. One sneaked through a window. Just imagine. He said he wanted to know the habits of people, that it would look well in a book! They put him on a prison treadmill and then they enlisted him in the English navy. He didn't have any stolen property on him. I think the story is in a book in this bookcase here."

The girl had gone pale as the lace-edged linens. But then she replied, "I could probably only afford an old book today. But I was wondering about this plate."

"Oh, that's Royal Cornwall china. It's their 'Life on the Western Prairie' series. They're not terribly expensive."

She examined the girl as the girl gazed from one plate to the next. Yes, she had seen her before. The girl might have been with the woman who sold the plates to her a few weeks ago.

"I might be back." The girl meandered towards the hallway and then Mrs. Butterstead could see her going to the stairs, her reflection in the art nouveau mirror and then the mirror with the girl fishing and then the floor mirror. It made Mrs. Butterfield feel more mystical than an antique dealer should be.

"Is your mother with you?" Mrs. Butterstead said, staying behind the girl who kept going on ahead of her. And then for a moment, they appraised each other as if they were both sensible of damages. Never having apprehended a shoplifter before, Mrs. Butterstead put her hand on the girl's arm. She clutched it, but because she didn't know what exactly to say, becoming confused she muttered "Adele."

The girl in the low-waisted shift fled like a specter to McDonald's where she ate an Egg McMuffin on her vacation savings. After that, she roamed until she came to a more well-to-do neighborhood. She felt like a free spirit, what her father was when he was young, her mother said. Lorna was lucky to run into a girl who chose her for squads at school. She was riding her bike and Lorna walked with her to her house and to the playhouse in her backyard. There, she told Renee about the old lady who she had escaped. She'd had to wear a dress to the antique house.

Out of the sun's interrogative glare, Lorna nearly fell asleep as Renee played with Kermit the Frog and Miss Piggy on her own stage. When Lorna didn't shriek at Miss Piggy toppling onto Kermit, she had to watch Miss Piggy pressing him and pinning him to the stage's proscenium. She had better be going. Renee's mother waved from a window above their hosta plants as Lorna ambled away, letting her basic sense of things direct her.

The sunshine was severe and Lorna, feeling horribly free, rambled on until she saw that her father's garage was open. The walnut furniture was no longer in the garage. Out of habit, she wandered into the kitchen where there were not only sandwich makings in the refrigerator but cans of pop for their vacation drive. The living room was clean and cool; the drapes were drawn. In the hallway, Lorna heard her parents' voices coming from their bedroom.

They heard her sandals on the stairs. None of this was ever going to happen again. As if they wanted to call those people with the playhouse. They would never be so hurting again, neither of them, none of them, ever. Lorna would never lie about where she was going and worry them again, would she? One bunking party at the women's shelter was enough for Lorna's mother. And her father was going to find someone besides an old bash buddy to talk with about his frustrations. They were planning to drive at dawn tomorrow morning. The last two days would be behind them.

For more work from Katherine L. Holmes, look for her short story collection *Curiosity Killed the Cat and Other Stories* from Hollywood Books International.

ELEANOR SWANSON

Stray Dogs

Comets ripped through the air. Kate opened a door. Water poured from the room in great waves. She stepped inside. Her husband Nick stood in the center of the room, drenched, wet sand at his feet. "You left me," he said. "I'm so lonely."

Nick got up before her and made coffee. She stared at him over the rim of her cup as he stood at the kitchen counter reading the newspaper and humming. In the dream, she had chosen to leave. Where had she gone? Nick glanced at her and smiled. "Want to hear some Irish music tonight? Over at the Bluebird Theatre?"

"Sure. What's the group?"

"Stray Dogs. Howard wrote a review of their last CD in that Celtic magazine he freelances for. I'll call and see if they want to go."

"Good idea," she said, dumping what was left of her coffee in the sink. Nick had made this morning's pot way too strong and her mouth was filled with its bitter aftertaste. Like the bitter past.

Nick came out of the bedroom still holding the phone. "I talked to Meg. Howard's at the grocery store. She wants to go, but she's going to have him call me when he gets back. She thinks he knows someone in the band."

"We can be groupies," Kate said. Fine. Something to do to take her mind off the fact that this was the fifth anniversary of Michael's death. No. The anniversary of the day they'd found his body.

"We can start getting in the mood for our trip to Ireland."

"I'm already in the mood." They were leaving in a few weeks. Nick would be spending a week near Galway checking out his company's new supplier of motherboards. He was an engineer. Who but a man would have named them that? "Motherboards," she said out loud.

"What about them?" Nick asked. She could tell he was hoping he could explain something about the inner workings of computers to her. He liked doing that. Explaining things came naturally to him. Quantum physics, gravity, paranormal occurrences.

"I just can't believe they're called that," she said. "Are there fatherboards? Babyboards?"

"There are daughterboards. Be logical," he said, with a hint of annoyance.

"No," she said, just as the phone rang. The world had already been invaded by too much logic. "I'll get it."

"I got all four of us on the guest list," Howard said when she answered the phone. "We can go backstage afterwards and meet everyone."

"You must have written a good review."

"I did."

"How did they get their name?"

"I haven't the slightest idea. You can ask them." There was silence on the line before he cleared his throat. "I know it's the time of year…," he hesitated. "Kate, I…"

"It's okay," she said, as tenderly as she could manage, but really wanting him to stop.

"I just wanted to let you know I was thinking about him too."

"Thanks, Howard."

She hung up and walked outside. Dirty clouds scudded west. Ominous, fantasy ships in an evil sea, as if conjured from some fable. Thunder sounded in the distance and the first drops spattered her legs and shoulders. She stood without moving as the rain gathered force. At first, the rain felt good. It had been fiercely hot no more than an hour ago. They hardly ever had this much rain in June. It hadn't rained like this since the summer Michael had drowned, rain day after day, until lakes lapped the high shore and rivers frothed at their banks.

"Kate," Nick called to her from the patio. "What are you doing?" His face showed a man yelling, but she could barely hear his voice through the pounding rain. Michael and Nick had set out on a kayaking trip Memorial Day weekend, to run Class V rapids in the Arkansas River. Somehow they'd become separated. There had been a search, but Michael's body hadn't been found until the middle of June. Rain rolled down her face and filled her shoes. Lightning struck in a white gash between the trees a yard away and she ran toward the house.

Nick was waiting with a towel. "What are you doing? Let's get inside."

Another bolt of lightning struck, and another. The storm was right over them.

Kate shook off the towel and walked away. She'd expected Nick to say something, to remember. "I need a shower," she said.

They sat in the Bluebird Theatre. It had recently been refurbished into a small concert hall, and it retained the worn charm of the old movie house it had been. But for the last few years before its remodeling, the only movies the Bluebird had shown were porn films. As they sat in the bronze glow of the stage lights, she thought of the couples writhing on screen –

nakedness, lust, and sweat. When the house lights dimmed, the chatter around them quieted.

The band was being introduced by a woman in a long flowered skirt. Kate tried to pay attention, but the woman's voice soon turned to a drone. *Support folk...music...lucky to have. Ireland*, she said. *Just in from Galway.* She waved her hand magically and the velvet curtains drew back. "Stray Dogs," she half-shouted before she withdrew. The applause was hearty and the mandolin kicked off the first tune. The tin whistle player stood half in shadow, his fingers busy. She watched as he shook his head slightly to throw back a shock of dark hair fallen into his face. She shivered at the gesture, and watched as he stepped forward into the light to take a break. Nick turned to her and took her hand.

Silence fell around her, palpable as the rain she'd stood in this afternoon. She had traveled out of time, and there was Michael, back from wherever he'd been. Finally, the aching for him could subside. She needed to go to him. She put her hands on both arms of her seat and felt herself starting to rise. She felt supernaturally strong, as if she could fly...but suddenly the tune was over and her hands were in her lap. Numbly, she raised them out in front of her and put them together. Nick touched her arm and she forced herself to look at him.

"They're good," he said, smiling.

Nick and Michael were both excellent athletes, strong swimmers. They'd been best friends for years. Even before Kate and Michael had become engaged, the three of them went backpacking and climbing, mountain biking, rafting. She was strong and fit, but they outmatched her. And by choice, she often stayed behind, working on her dissertation. "You don't blame me, do you?" Nick had asked in different ways again and again. She had reassured him each time, so logically, so calmly. She didn't blame him. She looked down at her chest, seeing her heart beating outside her body. She had lied, and Nick had become her consolation. And it had seemed to everyone that she'd been so calm, had returned to life so easily, going on with her work. *You're so strong. How do you do it?* She went on as if nothing had happened, while some small creature inside of her screamed out in grief.

Kate sensed without really quite hearing it that the music was good, very good. People smiled and clapped and tapped their feet in time. She heard, "Flowers of the Forest," a tune, announced, a solo, and Michael stepped forward and began to play the Uilleann pipes. The sound filled her. He played so sadly, so sweetly, that she felt borne on the air like a winged seed.

After the concert, they followed Howard backstage and he introduced them to the band. Brendan, lead singer and guitar player, Gavin, bouzouki, and the piper with the dark hair was Jamie. He held her hand instead of shaking it and looked into her eyes for a few seconds as he spoke. He was not Michael's twin, merely his double. She stared back, stunned.

"So it's Kate, is it? Are you Irish, Kate?"

"My great-great-grandfather on my father's side."

"So he left durin' the famine, like everyone. Where was he from?" He let go of her hand and reached into a duffel bag lying on the floor. He pulled out a pack of cigarettes, lit one, and waited for her answer.

"County Clare," she said, though she had no idea. She remembered only that Galway was in County Clare.

"How do you like that," he said a laugh. "And have you ever been?"

"We'll be there at the end of the month." She felt herself trembling.

"Is that so?" He jerked his thumb toward where the others stood. "With Nick, is it?" He threw his cigarette on the floor and stubbed it out with a heavy shoe. "Promise me you'll visit."

"I will."

"You're a darlin'," he said, and then looked away. "Hey mates!" he called. "Let's find a pub. I've been too many hours without a Guinness."

The pub was downtown, just a few miles from the Bluebird. Kate and Nick arrived first and waited outside for the rest. Nick stood on the step below her. They had married and no one had been surprised. After Michael disappeared, Nick had been the one to call her with the news. For days, he'd searched along the river with the others – sheriff's department, volunteers. When the search was finally called off, he came to her apartment and wept. He spent the night on the couch and slept most of the next day. She looked at his shoulders now, remembering how they had shaken with sobs and how she had taken him into her arms, finally, and tried to comfort him.

Nick turned to her, his face drawn and somber in the half-dark. "No one could have missed it," he said.

Kate was sure she heard bitterness in his voice just as she was sure of what he was going to say next. *Jamie looks like Michael.* But before he could say anymore, someone touched her shoulder and she turned.

"It's a real Irish pub, is it?" Jamie stood near her. He smiled.

Nick answered. "Everything was brought from Ireland," he said with a vague gesture toward the door. He came to stand at their level.

Gavin and Brendan appeared from around the corner.

"Let's get a table," Nick pointed inside, and they followed him into the bar.

She trailed behind them, catching the scent of woodsmoke and tobacco. Woodsmoke. Clothes after a backpacking trip, sleeping bags. Bits of ash still clinging to cooking pots and plates. Once, when they were in the Sangre de Cristos, the three of them, they'd been caught in a lightning storm while they were climbing Crestone Peak. Michael was in the lead. Nick was about two hundred yards below them. A bolt struck near them. Nick had screamed. She'd closed her eyes then. Fear ran through her with such stinging force, she imagined she'd already been hit. When she'd opened her eyes seconds later, Michael had been beside her, calmly urging her up the mountain. Somehow they'd climbed past the storm, ascending while Nick had scrambled down. "I'll never leave you," Michael had said, when they lay side-by-side at the top of the peak.

"Kate...," Howard, out of breath, was beside her. "They were fantastic, weren't they?"

"They were," she said, shivering. "It's cold in here. Where's Meg?"

"She dropped me off. She was getting a headache. Can I catch a ride home with you?"

"Sure."

At the table, Howard ordered a round of Guinness. She found herself between Jamie and Gavin. Gavin had a big face and close-set dark eyes. He pulled intently on his Guinness until the glass was half-empty. Traces of the creamy foam clung to his upper lip. He rubbed his mouth with the back of his hand. He looked at her. "You and your mate are coming over to Galway, are you? That's what Jamie here tells me. Is it true, Jamie?"

She felt Jamie's eyes on her and she turned and found his face close, as if he had been staring into her hair. "She said she would. She swore."

Gavin laughed softly and stared into his empty beer glass. "You're one of a kind," he said.

"Ah, I hope so," Jamie said, his eyes still on Kate. He pulled a pennywhistle from his pocket and began to play. Silence fell around them as his fingers flew upon the little flute, the length and back. When he was finished, he stood up and bowed. People near them applauded. "It's called 'The Strayaway Child,'" he said.

When he sat down, his breath was warm at her ear. "When you get to Ireland, I'll take you walking on the Burren," he whispered. "And we'll find him."

Galway.

Dublin had been a blur of enraged drivers and honking horns. She looked at bullet-riddled buildings and felt the Livvy flowing through her – water cleaving a heart. She opened her eyes. The hotel room was dark, quiet. Nick had disappeared before first light, picked up by a company car that would take him to the eastern outskirts of Galway where the factory was. Call Jamie, he'd told her last night. I won't be back to the hotel until late. That was the plan they'd agreed on at the pub in Denver, over a last pint. A plan, sealed with a handshake. We'll see you in Ireland, then. She got out of bed, walked to the window and drew back the heavy curtain. Fog. So heavy, she couldn't see across the courtyard. It was nine-thirty. Too early to call a musician, wasn't it?

She picked up the phone and dialed.

"Cheers."

Was it Jamie? "Hello," she said, her voice snagging on the second syllable.

"Is it you, love?"

"It's Kate," she said. "From Denver."

"Here to find the strayaway child, are you?" He laughed.

She imagined him speaking through the fog, obscured by dense clouds that lay across the water.

"I'll pick you up in an hour," he said, not waiting for an answer. "We'll walk the Burren and look for stories. Some call it a magical spot of land."
They stood at the edge of the sea. Jamie walked closer to the water, and closer, until a wave lapped over his scuffed work boots. He took another step until, halfway to his knees, his jeans were dark with the sea.

"What are you doing?" she called over the sudden wind.

He turned and faced her, shouting. "When you're a hungry ghost, you don't know what world to live in. Figure it out. Human lovers and dead ones. Stray dogs and strayaway children." He gestured toward the white-capped expanse of sea that lay before him. "They're all here." He thrashed through the pounding surf. A wave broke over him, and he was gone.

She ran. The icy water billowed in her clothes. She gasped for air and struggled to keep above the breaking waves. "Michael," she screamed. "Michael!"

When he leapt from the water and pulled her to him, she was not surprised, for she had called him. He wrapped his arms around her and they kissed.

She struggled her way up from the bottom, the water dark as blood. She was drowning. Someone took her hand and she opened her eyes. She lay in a strange bed.

"You're an odd one," Jamie said, "swimmin' in the Irish Sea in your clothes. I paddled out to get you like the stray dog I am, and I took you in me teeth." He growled softly. "Like this, he said, shaking his head from side-to-side. "Like this I saved you from meetin' your fate." He picked up his tin whistle and played three notes. "The Strayaway Child," he said. "Brought home."

For more work from Eleanor Swanson, look for her short story collection *Exiles and Expatriates* from Hollywood Books International.

NONFICTION

DONALD DEWEY

Blind Newsy Sees

The quickest way to show how inept you are is to work for a blind man. I learned this lesson at high school age when my blind uncle sometimes asked me to cover Friday afternoons at his newsstand, so he could catch an early train or plane for weekend frolicking.

Uncle Johnny's newsstand was in the lobby of a federal building in downtown Brooklyn. The lobby was always teeming with people either doing business at the ground-floor post office or taking elevators to the upstairs courtrooms for trials of murderers, Communist spies, and major tax evaders. It wasn't odd for trial defendants (with or without guards) to stop off at the newsstand on their way upstairs and, while they were waiting for the Life Savers or Juicy Fruit that would help get them through the next few hours, glimpse headlines predicting they were about to be sentenced to prison for the rest of their lives. I didn't care about the prison part. My worries were about the Life Savers and the Juicy Fruit.

To compensate for his lack of sight, my uncle set his wares over two enormous counters, two display cases, and various wall racks in a meticulous coded arrangement that would have stirred envy from the New York Public Library. His main improvement on the Dewey Decimal System was that he dispensed with the call numbers. The candy and gum, for instance, might have been logically enough in the stand's candy and gum areas, but that was like saying they were in the appropriate annexes of Willy Wonka's factory. Beyond that, and with a waiting customer tapping his foot for reasons other than being musical, any bumbling substitute vendor was on his own pawing at the chocolate bars that occupied one row, the hard candy tubes that occupied the row below, and the chunky mound things that occupied the one above. The key to the system, as Johnny could have told anyone he had felt moved to tell, was not alphabetical order, assortments next to their constituents going solo, or the separation of the suckables from the chewables, but feel. When he reached down to the third row in his candy section, he expected to distinguish the flatter surface of the plain Hershey from the lumpier almond kind the next box over. It was the fools with 20-20 vision who created confusion every time they went for the Chuckles and came up with the Dots.

But at least the candy and gum were displayed openly enough for most customers to do their own reaching before paying. That wasn't the case with the cigars and the cigarettes, numerous enough to send a surgeon-general screaming into an alternate universe. The cigars were exhibited under glass with the box tops open and facing the customer. This would not have been remarkable except for the sloppy practice of manufacturers to advertise their brand name on the inside of the top, which was also facing outward to the customer. The result was that reaching down from behind the lid could easily turn into a game of non-blind man's buff – a game that became especially thrilling when a customer forgot he had an index finger for pointing. A terse "two White Owls" without accompanying gesture could lead to a scramble through the whole bird kingdom before landing on the right box. This wasn't a problem for Uncle Johnny, of course. Since he had decades of sales figures in his head, he knew the White Owls, Muriels, and other big sellers deserved pride of access right inside the sliding door at the back of the display cabinet while the premium-priced specials from countries he had never heard of belonged in the extreme front to the extreme left where his hand seldom traveled. Unfortunately for inferiority complexes, when there was the random request for one of these specials, he got to it with a swiftness suggesting he hadn't anticipated anything else.

The thirty-odd cigarette brands posed a different challenge. Bottoms protruding, these were stacked in vertical slots behind the counter. This allowed for a comparative study of manufacturing lot numbers, but otherwise the package bottoms had only one thing in common – they didn't identify the brand for anyone except the quality control people back in North Carolina. Granted that with some practice you could remember that only a dozen brands printed the lot numbers in red while all the others used black, but as retail aids went, this wasn't much. None of this mattered to Uncle Johnny, either. He stacked them into the slots ass backwards because he insisted it was easier to slide them out that way on their cellophane wraps. It was a topic he really wasn't ready to debate, least of all for the argument that showing the tops might have permitted instant identification of the brand. Beneath what might seem like whimsical stubbornness was his profound belief that people with vision also had to learn to live with their handicaps.

As for the order of the stacking, it started off plausibly, with Camels, Lucky Strikes, and the other people's choice brands occupying the slots closest to the front of the stand. But then, somewhere in the vicinity of the menthols, the hit parade buckled. Once again, the key was the feel – specifically, the L&M box that marked off the bestsellers to its left and the also-rans for several stacks to its right. Where was the L&M soft pack? Several more files down because it had its own divider responsibilities with the boxes of other brands Madison Avenue was promoting as crush-proof. Why had L&M been given this mediation role in both cases? Both hard and soft, its cigarettes came in slightly taller packages, meaning it stuck out more from the cabinet files, meaning it hit Johnny's hand tellingly when he did a quick swipe over the cabinet, meaning he could get to some brand not in the Top Ten to the left or right of it faster.

Then there was the money. The coins presented no difficulty for Johnny because he wore a belt changer that had tactile safeguards against quarters trying to slip into nickel slots and nickels trying to fit into dime slots. The belt changer and I got along fine as long as I remembered that it worked like a gun – all squeezing, no jerking. What a jerk inevitably got the jerk was a bottom ring stuck one-third out with an unreleased coin, a finger bent on freeing the nickel or dime, and the ring seizing the finger with the disapproval of a bear trap as it dropped the coin and slid back into its metallic groove. In mundane practice, I had a big edge on Johnny on bills, but that also left me standing outside another part of the system he seemed to have worked out during a congress of Talmudic scholars. If the transaction involved only the passing of a bill for an item less than a dollar, no doubts or disputes: the assumption was that the dead president was George Washington. If the transaction was for less than a dollar and the customer helpfully declared "out of ten," Johnny repeated "out of ten" and one of the lobby guards usually hanging around the stand sauntered over to say that the Yankees needed more pitching. In guard talk this meant the customer wasn't a would-be conman.

Needless to say, there were times the Yankees could have found all the pitching they wanted from Johnny's customers. One journeyman of the game, for example, tried to pass a single off for a twenty and was immediately escorted to the main door with a warning not to come back unless it was to be tried upstairs. Another wiseguy, apparently more prone to receiving than kicking when he played football, handed over two singles, then claimed one of them was a ten and asked for it back. What he hadn't foreseen was Johnny's rigorous delegation of pocket tasks – the left pants pocket receiving only twenties, the right pants pocket only tens, the left duster pocket open only for fives, and the right one accepting only singles. When a ten didn't come out of the right duster pocket, the guards had somebody else to escort to the street. If there was no guard around when Johnny had serious suspicions about a customer, he resorted to the simple expedient of saying he couldn't change the big bill being declared.

Taking such an out was no easy compromise for my uncle because it reminded him of his physical vulnerability. He didn't like the reminder, not after years of denying any such frailty, including eschewing the use of a seeing-eye dog or cane. In their place he had developed another personal system for getting around – counting his steps. Only history's earliest map makers matched his nerve, ambition, and reliance on primitive mathematics. When he went off to work in the morning from the apartment he shared with my grandmother, his meter marked the number of paces down to the corner, up the three blocks to the subway, and down the stairs to the train. Inside the train he was one of those obnoxious linemen who blocked the door, in his case because his regimen demanded that when he arrived at his station in downtown Brooklyn, he restart the meter from the door to the street staircase as precisely as possible. Despite the normal commuter crowds in the morning, the last lap back up on the street was usually the easiest stretch because of the probability of running into someone headed for his building. That left him with the final task of discouraging his found companion from favoring either the tortoise or the hare so his own moderate tempo wouldn't be jumbled.

The paces of others were just one of several irksome drawbacks to the steps system. Another annoyance was when Johnny ran into an acquaintance on the subway platform who distracted him from his calibrations about where he was with snooping questions about how he was. Higher on the irritation scale were cops or firemen who didn't understand why he wasn't quick to obey their orders to detour from some accident or fire site. Higher still were those who took the absence of a dog or cane as evidence he was lying about his blindness. On one occasion, this led to being hauled off to a station house for trying to disguise his pimping; on another, for being the lookout for a grocery store robbery taking place two doors away from where he was waiting for a bus. One constant of all these misadventures was that the more outrageous they were, the more he relished recounting them at holiday family gatherings with a Presbyterian in one hand and a cheese-covered cracker in the other. The neighbor he had run into on the train platform would always be a serious menace for his commuting, but the cops who had run him in as a heist lookout would always be the stuff of hilarious anecdote. It was in line with this same trajectory that he never tired of relating his single most humiliating moment. That was the evening he had come up from his normal subway stop during a violent snowstorm, had to wander more to the left than he normally did because of drifts, and had begun noticing that the steps he was counting were getting hillier and hillier. He had halted that night only when a cop had yelled for him not to trudge another step through the snow or he would fall off the roof of the car he had just climbed.

But occasionally flawed as they were, Johnny's programmed solutions to daily tests saw him through. At the stand, the magazines were flanked in a wall rack from the costliest down to the cheapest so that most customers shorter than basketball centers betrayed a grunt going up for what they wanted. Each pile of newspapers – and there were plenty of dailies in New York at the time – had its own plastic change tray, making that part of the stand look like Woolworth's crockery department. When there were too many coins clanging other coins instead of a plastic bottom, it was the cue to empty the tray and retire the nickels and dimes to the belt changer. About the only commodity to daunt Johnny was a tree of paperbacks a distributor talked him into carrying, however briefly. The problem wasn't his inability to negotiate their varying prices; he devised a system of razor-nicking the tops of the covers, the placement of the cuts from the spine over to the edge marking the cost category. More troublesome was that he had to stick the tree at the back of the stand where it blocked his already-narrow passage for getting out from behind the counter to go to the bathroom or just stretch his legs. "I'm spending half the day crawling around the floor picking up the goddam things," he grumbled after his second collision. "People want to read books, let them go to the library." The paperbacks lasted less than a month.

Johnny's agility hardly went unnoticed. It wasn't rare for a customer to stand back after a purchase and dare the blind man to pull the same trick with the next person to come along. Many recounted their change in disbelief it was correct. For all the help they supplied at critical junctures, the guards also frequently assumed the role of fascinated spectators. (One exception was a security man who thought nothing about trumpeting to one and all "it's no big deal – you're blind, you get used to it.") This isn't to suggest my uncle was the only blind news vendor in the city; on the contrary, since the days of Franklin Delano Roosevelt, federal statute had given priority for such jobs to veterans and the handicapped. But because of his location, he managed to attract extra attention. If a trial upstairs hit a lull, for instance, leaving reporters to meander around while they chewed their gum flavorless, a profile of the newsstand operator broke the monotony. Invariably, unimaginative headline writers at the copy desk bannered the article with some variation on "Blind Newsy Sees............"

Then there were the celebrities who offered other kinds of exposure. For the most part, the Leo Durochers, Danny Kayes, and Barbara Stanwycks were in the building in connection with a court case, either as defendants or as witnesses. Their stop-offs frequently got them into enough conversation to reveal Johnny's encyclopedic knowledge of sports, theater, and movies. If it was sports, he could recall in elaborate detail when Babe Ruth had been a pitcher for the Red Sox, a slugger for the Yankees, and a bum of a coach for the Dodgers. Show business was a journey back through the Berts – Williams in vaudeville, Wheeler in the movies, and Lahr on the Broadway stage. Few of the notables remained unimpressed, and they contributed their own little tales while judges upstairs and other customers at the stand waited. Fairly regularly, they also went off to their legal appointments with promises to send tickets for this game or that performance. Most of them delivered, and I benefited from it as much as anybody.

As a rule, Johnny confined his socializing to the weekends – hitting a neighborhood bar with a cousin or a friend from childhood on Friday nights, a Manhattan restaurant with a girlfriend he had met at the Lighthouse for the Blind on

Saturdays, and another restaurant in Sheepshead Bay with the same woman on Sunday afternoons. A few times a year, there were also the bowling tournament trips organized by the Lighthouse in places like Omaha and St. Louis. During week nights, however, his regular companions weren't always available even if it meant, as it often did, orchestra seats in a Broadway theater compliments of the latest actor who had been dragged into court by the Internal Revenue Service. Those were the days I had to do my homework as soon as I returned home from high school, so I would be free in the evening to be an escort.

As adventurous as they might have been to me, Times Square's neon marquees and billboards on a weekday night might have been just an extension of the newsstand for Johnny, a part of his system that had preceded us over on the subway from Brooklyn. All he needed was the name of the theater we were passing to recite its history back to the Barrymores, Cornells, and Cohans. Titles of plays that hadn't lasted more than a week weren't his strong suit, but he hadn't forgotten how he had laughed at "the one where they drop all the plates on the butler in the first act" and cringed at "the one where the saloon girl falls in love with the cop who's always trying to roust her." He might not have remembered the actors who had played the butler and the saloon girl, but I remember it was on these outings that I saw that the likes of Paul Newman, Sidney Poitier, and Geraldine Page had existences outside of celluloid and that Arthur Miller, Tennessee Williams, and Eugene O'Neill weren't just classroom names for a study of Great American Plays. Not to say that there weren't discomfiting moments. Drug addiction, abortion, and castration weren't Bert Lahr, and every time they emerged as a salient plot point, Johnny shifted uneasily in his seat in admission of his moral turpitude for exposing the teenager to their existence. But almost always his verdict was the same on the trip back home: "Some rough stuff there, but the actors were damn good."

Where the actors weren't always damn good, on the other hand, was in the movies. For years, Johnny had caught every major feature that wasn't a western, a slapstick comedy, or something else that accented action over dialogue. His steady movie-going otherwise was an implicit testament to how basically stagy most Hollywood films were – schematic setups, tit-for-tat dialogue exchanges, and redundant on-screen references to what the characters were doing or about to do. Conversely, when my uncle began complaining that "nobody talks anymore!" and "what the hell are these people doing now?", it was more instructive than any Martin Scorsese lecture that movies were doing a lot more moving than they once had. From there it was an inevitable decision for Johnny to go to movies less and less frequently since "people don't say anything interesting anymore."

What he could never do without, on the other hand, was the radio. Music, ballgames, proto-talk shows – he monitored them practically through his every waking hour, at the stand as well as at home. In his later years of retirement, when Sinatra might have been confused for the name of a new automobile and the talk shows had evolved from the proto- to the paleo-, he was given to calling it "screwball radio," but he continued listening. And yet it was also radio that most strikingly marked Johnny's reach beyond total dependence on what entertainment the mass media had to offer. When he went to Ebbets Field or the Polo Grounds, or later Shea Stadium, he relied exclusively on the play-by-play of his companion. Asked once by my father why he never carted along one of the numerous portable radios he kept in his bedroom to keep better abreast of what was going on, he growled "that wouldn't be going to the game, I may as well stay home." Then he had his own question: How much of a lead was the runner taking off the base?

RICHARD THIEME

I Remember Mama

I remember my mother talking on the telephone.

She sat on the telephone bench in the hallway, turned toward the wall. She always talked loudly, as if what she had to say had been compressed and forced itself out of her. Energy sprayed out around the telephone like water from a garden hose ill-fitted to a spigot. Her laughter sounded like artillery fire, making me wince, and somehow she would still be laughing when she began her next sentence. Her need to connect with her friends was relentless, but they always seemed to remain just out of reach; she would no sooner finish one call than she made another, reaching out incessantly through the coiling black cord of the telephone toward someone's distant voice.

I knew there were others on the line. When she paused, which was not often, I could hear their little voices in the receiver at her ear. They sounded tiny and far away, a collection of toys like the big box of metal soldiers in my bedroom, or like Lilliputians, while she was Gulliver – if you can imagine Gulliver sitting on a telephone bench in a filmy nightgown, open turquoise robe, and turquoise mules with pompons on the tops.

Of course, this is just a broad outline. Later I would fill in details, working in from the brittle edges of her life: the reasons behind her hair-trigger readiness to snap back before the other voice had finished a sentence or the way her eyes jerked rapidly back and forth while she waved her cigarette in the air, not in time to any music. Perhaps this is how an artist sketches an outline and then fills in details, discovering progressively the receding depths of his subject.

I never could draw, but I do know how to remember.

As she finished a call, she'd have the telephone in her hand, flipping through her address book and dialing with her free hand while she balanced a cigarette above the cup of coffee on her knee. The saucer caught more ashes than the glass ashtray from the Fountainebleu Hotel on the ledge beside the telephone. I didn't know then that, unable to sleep, she tranquilized herself with sedatives, which put her so deeply asleep she couldn't go to work in the morning unless she roused herself with a different pill. Nor did I know that my mother's struggles would translate into mine as well but with a different flavor, different obsessions, different addictions.

The contours of our lives spill out of the cornucopia of time in surprisingly concentric circles, our patterns of behavior, from generation to generation, as self-similar as fractals. To see that pattern – to see ourselves wholly ourselves and the spitting image of our parents or our children – is healing. To see clearly the boundaries of our lives – our real place in the scheme of things – is the definition of integrity, humility, and peace. That's why I won't reduce this story to a catalog of details documenting the dysfunction of my family. I am not writing a case history nor am I engaged in self-examination prior to confession. Besides, every family is also a functional family, it all depends on where you are on the continuum and who defines the notches. These are the details, but if there were nothing but details, there would be nothing to write toward. I am writing always toward the possibility of glimpsing that fractal pattern; I am writing toward light, toward the intimation of a self or soul that will not be utterly obscured by the details of my life, toward a distant star looking as the sun must look from the orbit of Pluto.

I am writing toward home, listening for a signal.

The telephone fills the foreground of my memories of my mother. It looks huge, and I see her peeking around it, looking for the other pieces of her life. I learned to listen closely to how she sounded on the telephone, because it told me what to expect next. If she'd had a run of energizing conversations, she would return to the dining room table talking, the giddiness of her momentary excitement spilling over like the cup of coffee she carried back to the table too quickly. She would then play solitaire, smoke, drink coffee, and watch television across the table where she also spread out the newspaper, writing paper and pens, and various personal records, and where she placed the bicycle-backed playing cards in wide columns and rows. Smoke hung in the air between the glass chandelier and the crowded table. As she lay the cards on the plastic cloth, she maintained an energetic conversation with me, in a way, even if I was not in the room, and the television, which kept her company and whose stars sang to her and made her laugh or, sometimes, cry, and with herself, although she was usually too busy listening to the television to respond. If Jan Pierce sang "Bluebird of Happiness," or Eddie Fisher let loose with "O Mein Papa," my mother would freeze, her hands holding the deck of cards in mid-air, like one of those tragic figures buried in the ash at Pompeii, suspended forever in the midst of an incomplete gesture, until the song finished. Then she exploded. "Oh! God, that was powerful!" She literally vibrated in her chair, unable to contain herself, waiting for my brother or me to respond. We never knew what to say. Today, of course, I enjoy popular music, and when I drive in the countryside listening to "the hits of the sixties, seventies, and eighties," I am often transfixed. Alone in the car, the farms and fields passing outside the closed windows, I use the music like a drug. Then, however, I didn't know what to say, and her expectation that I would respond with emotion equal in intensity to hers would sooner or later give way to resentment. She sat up stiffly, snapping the cards with exceptionally crisp and deliberate precision, waiting for one of us to speak. After a while, one of us would say something to lance the tension – make a bad joke, ridicule the sentiment of the maudlin song, or just say something nasty – and she would burst into tears or explode with rage. She kept turning cards, moving aces up or playing from the deck, her back to our raised faces, showering us with shame and recrimination.

I don't remember what exactly she said; I only remember her

inexplicable rage. I discovered a metaphor years later for these outbursts when my mother-in-law, growing confused and forgetful, placed an empty coffee can in a microwave oven and watched, wide-eyed and frightened, while the oven erupted with arcs and sparks of white fire. Mom simply couldn't forgive us for not responding as grown men should.

Of course, we were not grown men; we were boys; but the absence of a grown man in the family blurred that distinction, and in the intensity of her need to have a grown man in the house, she conjured one up. We lived with him, that ghost who haunted our house more like a poltergeist than an insubstantial shade, although nothing flew through the air or crashed into the wall. Her wishes and desires commingled with a vague outline of our dead father to create a point like a Lorenz attractor against the power of which we were defenseless. We were drawn again and again toward a point always impossible to reach. Perhaps Hamlet lived with the same vague sense of an interrupted person always on the verge of coalescing into a genuine if imprecise expectation. I understand why Hamlet waited. It is difficult to model yourself after someone who has disappeared into thin air. The lack of form and clarity of his outline make it very difficult to color your own life entirely within the lines, although that very lack of definition creates an infinity into which to grow. Since no one is really there, you vacillate always between who you are and who you believe you are meant to be. You become a kind of ghost yourself, and the incongruity between self and sought self makes it likely that you will resemble your father, who is absent and present at the same time, more than you know.

My brother and I learned to do everything we could to be who we weren't. A high proportion of our energy flowed into letting go of ourselves and hoping we would coalesce on the other side. Is that what constitutes a haunting, a spirit giving everything it has to try to manifest itself in another dimension instead of just staying where it is? If so, my brother and I were also like discarnate spirits, seeking to manifest ourselves, to be present, to have an impact or make a difference, simply to show up somewhere and be.

Years later, we are still trying.

The telephone bench is where she came alive. That bench, a brown seat on a dark wood base, with a shelf for the telephone book under the black telephone, which itself sat on a ledge beside a pad of paper and a gold pencil, that telephone bench in the entrance hall of our apartment is the picture frame, elaborately carved and gilded, always containing the image of my mother.

It was also where she planned and carried on affairs. I remember her mouth pressed almost to the receiver, talking into the pores of the handset as if they were the very ears of the men with whom she connected. I felt the electricity in the air and the burning shame and sense of helpless grace before which I was abashed, like Moses before the burning bush. Emblems of the presence of God arrive in strange envelopes. Watching my mother make love with her voice and the language of her body to the telephone taught me something of God. Grace came later and gave me the strength and courage to realize with neither shame nor rage but with deep feelings of sadness and wonder that the forms in which God comes to us are always distorted by the memories, which make such a maze of our spiritual quests. It is a miracle that out of the smoke and fire of the battlefields of our lives we one day do emerge onto the plains of redemption.

Theodicy. The problem of evil, sickness, accidents, death. *Why do bad things happen to good people?* A masterful title for a bestseller! *Why do bad things happen to people?* would never have sold; none of us think we're just "people." The indifference and selfishness in our daily lives is shielded by the belief that we are good. The problem, of course, is not that bad things happen to good people, but that bad things happen to us.

My brother was five years old – I was two – when our father died. Our father had loved my brother very much, and when he died, the hole it left in my brother's life was huge. He remembers more vividly than I the sounds and sights of grief, lights burning at midnight, the telephone ringing, strangers milling about our living room, holding each other and crying, and he will remember always the well-intentioned aunt who told him God wanted his Daddy in Heaven. My brother, of course, immediately became an atheist, suggesting, I think, that atheism, at least some of the time, is the belief in a power greater than ourselves, which either does incomprehensible and hurtful things or simply refuses to show up. The God in which Arthur refused to believe is not a being who says "I am not," but one who says, "I will not." Given the evidence, Arthur's decision made sense.

Otherwise we were Jews, not very good Jews, but, still, Jews. The way one responds to the word "Jew" is what makes one a Jew. Being a Jew is not exclusively about tradition, religion, or culture. It is about the vibrations that resonate in your breast as if you are a tuning fork when the word "Jew" is sounded. When, as a child, you hear the word "Jew," regardless of whether it is said nicely or derisively, and you know they're talking about you, then you are a Jew.

Learning to be a Jew, then, means learning how to respond to people who think you're a Jew and treat you as a Jew, including yourself. Including God.

We went to a reformed synagogue on Rosh Hashanah and Yom Kippur. Twice a year we were pressed into a forced march along Lake Shore Drive in Chicago that we derisively called the "Zoo Parade." Hundreds of us marched up and down the street in what we believed was nothing but an effort to see and be seen. The twilight along the lake shore was a nocturne of shadows cast by street lamps, cool damp mist, and mink. Had animal rightists been around, they could have stood in blinds in the decorative shrubs that framed the lighted signs in front of apartment houses and mowed down the matrons who had caused the slaughter of so many hapless animals. The excursion was a ritual of mortification, which began when our mother powdered her face and rouged her cheeks and sprayed on so much perfume I expected visible mists to rise like fog from dry ice. The passenger elevator in our apartment building often retained her scent for hours; when I came home, I could tell if she had been there first, and if so, how long she'd been home.

It was eight blocks from our apartment to the synagogue, and as we walked, our mother examined the faces coming toward her through the evening, the ones coming home from the early service, ready to say hello. At the same time, she managed to keep us walking on either side of her, so we looked like the escorts she wanted us to be. We felt like wings without which she might spiral down through the air and crash. We hated having to hold her up, pretending to care about being greeted by people we barely knew. When she saw someone she recognized, I could feel a surge of enveloping warmth, which no one on the crowded sidewalk could easily resist. They had to nod and say hello. That "hello" was a validation stamped on all of our foreheads: you are here: and also a kind of searchlight that illuminated our inner being as the fluoroscope in the shoe store showed us the bones of our toes. As they passed in the night, our mother's eyes were already searching other faces, her smile held in readiness, waiting to flash. Between greetings, we walked in a kind of suspended animation, waiting for the next hello. People who passed without saying hello or who didn't know us barely existed. They were ghosts floating among real people. There were forty or fifty ghosts for every genuine human being. Those ghosts created vast amounts of interstellar space among tiny islands of brightness. During walks in the autumn night, we learned that people are real only when they're acknowledged. My mother's example was imprinted deeply on our souls; my brother and I grew up within a field of loneliness and longing that is like the descriptions I read of space/time wrinkled by ripples and dips of gravity. One cannot extract the thing itself from the field in which it occurs. Our essential selves are indistinguishable from the waves of distortion which make the others we encounter look like faces in the funhouse mirror of our own souls.

I sometimes think of that indelible lesson, learned during those long walks, when I watch my brother, a folksinger for many years, perform. He sits on a stool in the spotlight, mopping his forehead and cheeks with a red bandanna, looking out at the faces caught on the edge of the light. Their eyes are turned upward toward him, a reflecting pool in which he sees himself, and when he sings ballads and they applaud or tell jokes or tall stories and they laugh or groan, he is alive. His image is reflected back to himself clearly and with a minimum of distortion. From my seat beside the stage, the shadowy faces vague in the smoke and dimness of the distant reaches of the cafe look like shades in Hades. They indistinguishably blend into an ebb and flow of approbation, which uplifts and renews him. He sings and plays his guitar the way Mom said hello to the ghosts of the autumn night. In a dark cafe to which you have driven miles through rain or snow, eating a Big Mac while you stay focused on the lights of the oncoming traffic, it must always feel like an autumn night into which you walk alone, a frightened child stepping onto a huge vacant stage. Some nights, there are more than forty or fifty ghosts for every genuine human being.

I also thought of those walks when I became an Episcopal priest and celebrated the Eucharist or stood in the pulpit preaching. Sometimes it was deathly still, as if the members of the congregation had all inhaled and held their breath. At my best, I was deeply attuned to the personality of the congregation and could read feelings rippling through the crowd as an islander looks out at the ocean and reads the sea. I felt waves of anxiety or hospitality or affection, my antennae searching for the signals, which gave me the feedback I need. Then I followed the signals home.

I have been listening for a long time. Listening to my mother talking on the telephone told me what to expect next so reading feelings in the hearts of the faithful was not the hard part. Learning what to do with them is what took time.

In all the congregations I have served, my mother is alive. She sometimes wears disguises, but I always know when it's really her. I can feel the surge of enveloping warmth, the relentless need to connect, and the hopes and expectations, which can never be filled by any human being.

Knowing all that, and knowing so many other things as well, nevertheless, years later, I am still trying.

From one point of view, then, my brother and I both used traditions we had to learn – the world of American folk music in his case, the world of the Episcopal church in mine – traditions foreign to the obvious externals of our upbringing, to organize and somehow make sense of a history that is not even ours, except by proxy. We are branches grafted onto someone else's tree, adopted sons of imaginary fathers. By learning and telling the stories of other people's lives better than they can tell them themselves, we make their story ours. They become our brothers and sisters, children of one father who is present and absent at the same time.

I have watched my brother elicit patiently and with subtle effective diplomacy from a drunken drifter in a slum hotel the fragment of some song as if he will discover in the variant narrative something of himself. This history, which customers are in danger of forgetting, he remembers for the members of the audience. Their applause is an echo of the self he discovers as he sings, the bounce of a radar wave. On a good night, you can't tell where he begins and the audience ends. It is not that his boundaries are so blurred that he has no identity. On the contrary, he has discovered who he is, making a community for himself each time he takes out his guitar and sings.

The source of all communities, gathering for an evening like campers in a forest around a fire, are mixed motives issuing from the invisible point where the orbits of self and sought self almost touch.

As I said, that's one point of view. From another, we're still just two small boys, putting ourselves out there, making people say hello.

CURTIS SMITH

A Rusty Chain

I set my alarm for five o'clock on a Saturday morning. Groggy, my ritualistic shower skipped for fear of waking my wife and son, I shuffled through our house's predawn hush. My office is a converted porch, a chilled space that still retains the heavy wooden door that once sealed out the elements. The latch clicked a gentle goodbye when I shut the door behind me.

Waiting upon my desk was a story that had been vexing me for weeks. I blew steam from my coffee cup, slurped a tentative, tongue-burning sip. I dog-eared pages, scribbled ideas across the margins, layered the second scene in post-it notes. My highlighter squeaked as it painted the more-deserving passages in glowing pink. The story had started with promise, a seemingly coherent linking of images and events and characters, the dominos falling just as I'd imagined, but somewhere along the line, the calling voices had abandoned me. My vision blurred, and my faith evaporated with each new dead end. Still, the story pulled at me, a mysterious gravity buried deep in my gut.

Hours passed. The stark February sun reached into my office, and the view outside my window rose from the morning's murky grays. My closed door could only muffle the house's stirring activity for so long. The radio played the weak-signaled jazz station. My son jerked the unplugged vacuum over the hardwood floors, the plastic wheels clattering, the end tables' lamps shivering with each bump. I clamped my hands over my ears and, in a dry whisper, I read my story again. I was desperate to hear the passages anew, but I couldn't. Branded by familiarity, the words leapt into my thoughts before they passed my lips, and my head swam with nonsensical echoes. Ironic – that my absorption in my own fictional landscape also exiled me from it.

Frustrated, I rose from my desk and left my office. I needed a change of scenery, a setting not hemmed in by familiar walls. Ours is a family of few steadfast rules, but one is the necessity for a daily dose of fresh air. With the dual goal of clearing my head and getting my son out for a bit on what promised to be a rammy, indoor day, I decided the two of us would venture out for a hike on a nearby trail.

As I dressed my boy, I recounted our favorite trailside shenanigans. When his head popped through his sweater's neckhole, I wove stories of rumbling though leafless thickets. As I wrangled him into his boots and puff-tasseled cap, I helped him envision the bobbing of hurled twigs on the creek waters, which today would run swift with snowmelt; helped him hear the shivering notes made when our rocks broke the bank's clinging ice. On the ride, I reminded him of our visit just last weekend, how he'd run so fast I had to jog to keep up, retold the story of the slushy snowballs we'd packed and splattered against a sycamore's bark-speckled trunk.

I pulled into the trailhead's dirt lot. The previous week's thaw had passed and now winter had returned. A cutting breeze whisked off the creek. The cloudless sky ached a scintillating blue, and the cold and unforgiving light made all that surrounded me seem somehow brittle and just a breath shy of snapping. A thirty-yard path led to the woods. Unruly brambles bothered one side of the trail, the other guarded by a split-rail fence that separated the path from a scrub field. My boy and I moved slowly, our process hampered by our bundled layers, by the unobstructed, eye-tearing wind I hadn't counted on when I stepped out of the house, and perhaps it was this shuffling pace which allowed my son to fixate on a fence gap blocked off by a sagging length of chain. We'd passed this spot dozens of times without a thought or complaint, yet today my boy latched onto the chain with hands that had already shed their mittens. He shook the chain and smiled at the wood-clanking ripples he produced.

I picked up his mittens. The trees' bare branches clattered in the wind, and I worried about my son's winter-chapped skin. *Come on, bud*, I urged, but he ignored me. I took his hand, and on our walk into the woods, I trumpeted the treasures awaiting us. There would be squirrels to chase and sticks to snap. Perhaps we'd catch sight of the molting ducks who gathered on the debris-littered island halfway across the creek, their nests secreted away amid the upstream shore's collection of shopping carts and driftwood and bald tires. Pausing, I pulled his mittens from my pocket, an opportunity my boy seized to make an about-face dash back to the chain. Latching on with both hands, he swung the chain with a mischievous passion I had yet to fully recognize in him.

My boots crunching over the trail's snow patches and frozen mud, I joined my son. The chain clanked ferociously under his assault, a mesmerizing, humpbacked sway. I humored him, asked unanswered questions about the chain's chill and the coppery residue it left on his palms. An icy gust brought tears to my eyes. I nudged my boy's shoulder, and when he didn't budge, I gently yet firmly grabbed a fistful of his coat. With the touch, my boy sank into his jacket, that toddler-unique posture of every muscle in his body going simultaneously limp and rigid. Guilt found me; guilt for subjecting him to the brutal cold; guilt for denying him such a simple pleasure. I knelt by his side, insisting only he put back on his mittens. How strange his surroundings must have seemed to him sometimes, how immense, a universe waiting to be understood and so much towering overhead, so much out of reach, his mother and I the only bridges to the great, bustling mysteries that formed the backdrop of his days.

He resumed his shaking. Fearful that the writhing links would smack his chin, I held a protective hand near his face. A rail in the neighboring section of fence tumbled to the ground, and a glazed sense of pride filled his eyes. I studied him and the blurred chain, an exile once again in the realm of understanding and connection.

During my wife's pregnancy, we discussed purchasing a video camera. I did my research but was daunted by the cameras' slew of perplexing options, widescreen ratios and megapixels, the paramount question of High-8 or digital. Thanks to my feet-shuffling, my boy's birth and homecoming went unrecorded. Two more months passed before my internal dawdling reached its own sort of critical mass and, in an uncharacteristic rush, I drove to the nearest electronics store and returned home with a camcorder that offered a reassuring middling of features.

We started with two cassettes. One was for regular shots, spur-of-the-moment bursts of cuteness, visits from relatives. The other was devoted to clips intended to be taken at monthly intervals. Someday we would watch this tape, and surely its images would come back to us like echoes of a lost yet wonderful era. All I had to do was study the elementary school kids waiting for the bus on my corner to understand the fleeting nature of these first years, a time I knew was special yet was already blurred by the day-to-day changes in my schedule, the night awakenings, the doctors' appointments, and the weekend visits from grandparents and aunts and cousins anxious to nuzzle the family's newest arrival.

The first ten minutes on this tape consist of our boy doing little more than lying on his back. He wears his most darling outfits, the protracted scenes lingering due in part to our camera-wielding naiveté and, to a greater extent, our tardy epiphany – a realization fostered by the viewfinder's oddly detached perspective – that we now shared our days with this helpless yet completely autonomous creature. In these initial shots, our son spits and gurgles and kicks, his face glowing with saucer-eyed intentness. In the background, we coo and urge, our hands sometimes reaching into frame to dab his chin or to indulge ourselves in another caress of his pudgy cheek.

In the months to come, we would coax him to perform his tricks. Captured on that tape were his early efforts to sit up and roll over, to stack blocks and cruise around his crib. We recorded unsteady steps and the uttered syllables only a hopeful parent could decipher. And here, the tape underwent a distinct metamorphosis, for our staged events began to crumble beneath our son's unleashed sense of play and free will. See the boy run. See the boy fall. Hear our gasps and his daredevil's laughter. Somewhere around his second birthday, he discovered the wonders of the camera, and our tapes experienced yet another transformation, for now we couldn't unscrew the lens cap without being bumrushed, our shots fraught with images of us batting aside the hands that deposited peanut butter smudges across the lens. Look out!

Bedtime, and behind us were stories and snacks, roughhousing antics and nuzzling goodnight kisses. My fingers carried the flowery scent of the moisturizer I'd rubbed on his chapped cheeks. The unlaced hiking boots he'd worn that morning to the trail rested by his bed. At my boy's request, I sat in the chair in the corner of his room, my presence a comforting link between the day's bustle and evening's wind-down lull. My boy lay in bed, fighting the heaviness that pulled on his eyelids, his rump hoisted in a final, protesting posture. An inch from his nose, he pushed a tiny car, nudging it one way, then the other, the wheels turning in a hypnotist's back-and-forth sway.

I turned my attention back to the story that had so perplexed me that morning. Perspective had found me, and one by one, the jigsaw pieces of my rewrite fell into place. I jotted notes in a furious scrawl, and when I was done, I gathered the marked pages that lay fanned out around me. How easily manipulated, this fictional world, its spectrums of emotions and reactions molded by my desires alone. How false and how pretty and neat, these silent lives. An hour had slipped past, and while I'd been engaged, my son had drifted off, his fingertip resting on the car's trunk. Before leaving, I sat on his bed and pulled up the covers. I laid a hand upon his head, wondering if perhaps he'd dream that night of the trail's rusty chain.

I shouldn't have been surprised by my son's attraction to a rusty chain for his days were full of unintended playthings. There was the vacuum. The kitchen pots with their clanging lids. Our clock radios, which had a knack for going off at insane hours, the crackling volume pegged at full blast, the tuner set to static-garbled frequencies at the dials' ends. And add to this list of unexpected fun the boxy Polaroid he discovered one afternoon in the rear of our bedroom closet. We showed him how to squint with one eye and use the other to peek through the viewfinder. A few shots remained in the cartridge, and with a flash and a whir, out shimmied his first portraits. *Smile*, he echoed.

Buying him his own roll of film for our 35-mm was my wife's idea. His dawning excitement grew as we loaded the roll, his hand squeezing my knee as the automatic advance purred. He discovered the viewfinder on his own, and we guided his finger to the shutter button. Within the next five minutes, he snapped a dozen shots, my eyes swimming with the flash's burning afterimages. *Smile, Daddy. Smile, Mommy.*

With no warning, he set the camera down and rejoined the object of his morning play, a cardboard box delivered by the UPS man, its surfaces scribbled with markers and crayons, its sides perforated by a jabbing pen. *Poke*, he cried with each piercing. A week passed before I held the camera again. Unnoticed by either of us, our boy had finished snapping the roll's pictures.

My son had reached the cusp of a new brand of play. Much of his day was still occupied by frenzies of sprinting and leaping and box-stabbing mayhem, but now these bursts were interspersed with calmer, more intense interludes. Stretched out across the floor or kneeling beside the coffee table, he'd hunker down at eye level with his trains or cars or plastic animals. With a surprising delicacy, he positioned these toys, and as he maneuvered them, his perspective shifting as he framed the scenes in alternating points of view, he mumbled scenarios, serious-toned narratives that made me realize I wasn't the only one weaving stories under our roof.

With him thus engaged, I became free to settle near him, a witness to his initial forays into the realms of projection and reaction, the playacting of fictional landscapes and future relationships. These were the kinds of moments I wished I could capture on video, his first teetering steps in a lifelong crusade of trying to make sense of his world. And if he'd let me, I'd glide my fingertip across the flyaway strands of his curls, content to sit still and silent and tether my ramshackle, somewhat inelegant existence to such a beautifully fragile moment.

Another Saturday at the creekside trail. A new layer of snow coated the ground. The windshield intensified what little warmth the sun offered. I turned off the engine and cracked the window to listen to the water's rush. In the backseat, my boy was preoccupied with the ice scraper. He ran the bristles across his palm then under his chin, and I used this moment of repose to open the stiff photo envelope I'd just picked up from the drugstore.

There was a nice shot of his mother and me. A skewed picture of our steps that made them seem absolutely mountainous. Distorted close-ups of his trains. And then there were the confusing ones, blurry images I held one way, then another…close…then back…all in an effort to decipher what I was looking at.

I returned the pictures to the envelope and gathered the video camera I'd set on the passenger seat. With the carrying case slung over my shoulder, I helped my boy climb from the car. *It's cold*, he observed as I pulled his cap snug over his ears. When we reached the gravel trail, I let go of my boy's mittened hand and readied the camera. These days of simple wonders would soon fade, and I felt compelled to capture part of them, to steal them away from a past that disappeared quicker than the sticks we threw into the creek's deceptively swift waters.

My son trundled ahead, and I hustled to capture him in the viewfinder, the shadow of the split-rail fence like a mask across his eyes. *It's cold*, he repeated, only now he was smiling. The viewfinder's image jerked as I hustled to keep pace, but the trail's ruts and the split perspective of my eyes and the viewfinder's captured scene robbed my steps of any grace.

I crouched on the other side of the chain and framed my son. He latched on, but gone was the previous week's do-or-die intensity, his clanging today delivered more out of duty than glee. He released the chain and considered me, his breath pluming before his face. He picked up a nearby stick and walked down the path, whacking tree trunks and mowing down a swath of tan, scraggly weeds.

He stopped when I called his name. I held the camera, the scene witnessed from three unique angles. Unlike my writing or my son's playtime scenarios, there were no easily culled absolutes lingering beneath the surface, no tidy resolutions waiting to be plucked from the frigid air, yet I sensed a hint of truth – however vague and elusive – lay triangulated between our separate takes of this shared moment. As I approached, I encouraged him to wave. *Goodbye*, he said. With a button push, the viewfinder faded to black. My son turned and ran, his stick leaving a trail through the snow. *Come Daddy!* he cried. I zipped the camera back into its case and set out after him. How lovely, to have nor want any other choice than to follow in his wake.

DRAMA

DAVID-MATTHEW BARNES

It's a Pleasure to Be Sad

Cast of Characters

CATHY, 16. As the only daughter of a powerful Los Angeles businessman, she has let go of all edges of reality and has surrendered to a depression that has insulated her from the rest of the world.

DAWSON, 15. The only son of a working class family, he has never known luxury or love.

PLACE Cathy's overly decorated upstairs bedroom in an upscale house in the hills of Palos Verdes, California. A window in the bedroom offers a view of the city below where the Watts Riots raged two years ago.

TIME October 1967. A Thursday.

ACKNOWLEDGMENT
It's a Pleasure to Be Sad was developed in workshop at the 2007 Southampton Writers Conference in New York under the instruction of Marsha Norman.

From "Glad To Be Unhappy" as recorded by The Mamas and The Papas:

"Fools rush in, so here I am
Awfully glad to be unhappy.
I can't win, but here I am
More than glad to be unhappy.

Unrequited love's a bore, yeah,
And I've got it pretty bad.
But for someone you adore,
It's a pleasure to be sad."

(When the play begins, CATHY sits at her bedroom window, through which she stares intently at the horizon in the distance. Day quickly becomes night and flecks of the California sunset illuminate her face. She is dressed more for fashion rather than for comfort. Her hair is peroxide blonde; a little too styled, too big. Her eyes are prominent and outlined in heavy layers of black mascara and eyeliner. There is a permanent sense of defeat in her posture, as if she has given up on everything and sitting, standing, or speaking requires a tremendous amount of effort.

On a nightstand radio, the song "Glad To Be Unhappy" by The Mamas and The Papas plays at a low volume. CATHY hums along with the music as an afterthought. When she realizes that she is actually enjoying the song, she stops herself, stands, and goes to the radio. She shuts it off and contemplates reprimanding the radio, herself. She opens a drawer in the nightstand, places the radio inside of it, and shuts it.

There is a knock at the bedroom door.)

CATHY stares at the door with a sudden sense of panic, fear. She moves to the door, puts an ear against the wood. She listens for a second before speaking.)

CATHY: Who is it?

DAWSON: (from the other side of the door) It's me.

(CATHY opens the door at once. She pulls DAWSON inside and shuts the door before anything or anyone can follow him inside the bedroom.

DAWSON is boyishly handsome and possesses a blue collar charm. He wears a t-shirt, jeans, and a pair of old sneakers. His build is athletic but not intimidating.)

DAWSON: Your mother called me –

CATHY: You've been home for three days.

DAWSON: She said you were upset.

CATHY: You didn't want to see me?

DAWSON: We broke up, remember?

CATHY: But you've been gone all summer.

DAWSON: It was only six weeks.

CATHY: But it was Texas.

DAWSON: I went back to work the minute I got home.

CATHY: So soon?

DAWSON: I have to help my family out. You know that.

(She reaches for one of his hands. She holds it, stares at it.)

CATHY Do you think you'll be a dishwasher for the rest of your life?

(He pulls his hand away from her, burned.)

DAWSON: Your father stopped me when I came in the house.

CATHY: He thinks you're going to change my mind about Santa Barbara.

DAWSON: He wants to move to Santa Barbara?

CATHY: No. He wants me to go to school there. College.

DAWSON: He had a gun.

CATHY: He always has a gun.

DAWSON: A rifle.

CATHY: It's a shotgun. But it doesn't have any bullets in it.

DAWSON: Does he know that?

CATHY: It wouldn't matter if he did.

DAWSON: He said something to me.

CATHY: What did he say?

DAWSON: (he imitates her father:) The Army's gonna get you kid.

CATHY: He was on the phone earlier.

DAWSON: (terrified) With the army?

CATHY: No. With the emperor of Japan.

DAWSON: Do you think he could introduce me to Colonel Sanders? My Mom loves that guy.

CATHY: (she shrugs) My mother got a new car.

DAWSON: Another one?

CATHY: It's a blue thunderbird. She loves that thing more than…

DAWSON: She loves it because it's a Thunderbird?

CATHY: No. She loves it because it's blue.

DAWSON: She said you were sad. She said you weren't handling things…well.

CATHY: You broke up with me. You went to Texas.

DAWSON: I had no choice.

CATHY: I forced you to break up with me?

DAWSON: Texas. I had no choice about Texas. I had to go there and work. Help out my uncle.

CATHY: I keep forgetting you're not from California.

DAWSON: Is anybody?

CATHY: But you're back now.

DAWSON: Cathy, we broke up before I left.

CATHY: Are you still seeing what's-her-name? The girl with no neck.

DAWSON: Barbara.

CATHY: She used to be a friend of mine.

DAWSON: It's not her fault. I asked her out.

CATHY: Someone should have stopped you. Now you're stuck with no neck Barbara and I'm here all alone.

DAWSON: You're not alone.

CATHY: You're right. This is a big house. There's bound to be a ghost or two floating around here somewhere.

DAWSON: Your parents give you everything.

CATHY: That's because they blame each other.

DAWSON: For what?

CATHY: They hate each other.

DAWSON: No, they don't.

CATHY: They do, Dawson. They both think the other is a murderer.

DAWSON: What are you talking about?

CATHY: Before I was born. They had a son.

DAWSON: His name was Dennis, right?

CATHY: Let me guess. My mother told you about him.

DAWSON: In the garage. She had me bring some boxes down from the rafters. There were a lot of pictures of him.

CATHY: She has a shrine of him in her bedroom. She even had his little shoes bronzed. Like he was a living saint and everything he ever touched is sacred now. She thinks my father killed him. He thinks she was neglectful. It doesn't matter whose fault it was, the boy is dead.

DAWSON: How did he die?

CATHY: Technically, it was suicide. Well, no. It started out as suicide but it turned in to murder...an accidental murder.

DAWSON: Your father did it, didn't he? Was he shot?

CATHY: Dennis did it to himself. He was only three years old and he already knew…he knew what this house was like. This family. He went out to the garage and found poison. Strong stuff. The kind of stuff that kills snails and slugs in the garden. He ate a bunch of it. If you ask my father, it's because my mother had taken one too many tranquilizers for the day. According to her though, he was too busy buying more stock to notice that Dennis had slipped out of sight.

DAWSON: Did they take him to the hospital, or did he die here?

CATHY: No. It was the hospital that killed him. They were supposed to pump his stomach…but they accidentally filled his lungs. He was drowning and no one knew it.

DAWSON: No one could save him?

CATHY: He was too young to know how to swim. (Beat.) No one's been the same since.

DAWSON: But you weren't even born yet.

CATHY: But they had me soon after. Like they needed to make up for something. Time, maybe. It was in all the papers when he died. They made a big deal about it. The son of a pharmacist dies of poisoning. It was…shocking.

DAWSON: Cathy, your Mom told me something.

CATHY: About the blue Thunderbird?

DAWSON: She said I needed to come and see you. She said she was worried that you might do something to yourself…hurt yourself somehow.

CATHY: Well, if I did…I'm sure they would never bronze my shoes or sue the doctors. They would blame it on something else.

DAWSON: Love?

CATHY: You say the strangest things sometimes.

DAWSON: I wasn't going to come and see you.

CATHY: I know.

DAWSON: Not until your mother called me.

CATHY: I know.

DAWSON: You and I…we're different. We don't come from the same place.

CATHY: But we go to the same school.

DAWSON: My mother works three jobs.

CATHY: Does she have to?

DAWSON: No. She only needs one. But I think she prefers to be away from the house.

CATHY: Because of your father?

DAWSON: Because I think she wants more than what she got.

CATHY: Is that why you broke up with me? Just because my mother doesn't work?

DAWSON: I believe your mother does work. Taking care of you keeps her very busy.

CATHY: It's my father who makes her do everything. He can't get by without her.

DAWSON: Barbara comes from my neighborhood.

CATHY: So. That doesn't mean anything.

DAWSON: But I heard things. Before I went to Texas.

CATHY: Whatever you heard, it wasn't true.

DAWSON: Maybe it was.

CATHY: Who told you? Pam? Shelly? Chuck? You can't believe a word he says.

DAWSON: I heard stuff down at the beach.

CATHY: You never go to the beach.

DAWSON: But you do.

CATHY: I like to surf.

DAWSON: A lot of people say you're good at it.

CATHY: I am.

DAWSON: Even though you're a girl.

CATHY: That means nothing.

DAWSON: I heard stuff about you and some of the boys down there.

CATHY: What boy?

DAWSON: Not just one boy.

CATHY: I know a couple of guys down there. So what. I'm not married yet.

DAWSON: Eddie?

CATHY: I spent some time with him.

DAWSON: Were there others?

(She goes to the window, sits.)

CATHY: A few.

DAWSON: Even when we were together?

CATHY: Yes. (Beat.) Even then.

DAWSON: Yeah. That's what I thought.

CATHY: Do you know what the name of the street means? The street I live on. Via el Sereno.

DAWSON: No. But it sounds Spanish.

CATHY: It is. It means the night watchman.

DAWSON: How do you know that?

CATHY: I took Spanish class, dummy. Remember?

DAWSON: Oh yeah. But that was last year, wasn't it?

CATHY: I think it's strange that this street is named for a night watchman.

DAWSON: Maybe they named it that because of the view. How you can see the entire city from up here.

CATHY: Not the entire city.

DAWSON: No, but most of it.

CATHY: I remember when the city burned. Two years ago. It was August. Before you and I met that September.

DAWSON: Oh yeah. The riots.

CATHY: I could see it from here. The fire. The people looked so small. Like dolls in a doll house. Like someone – a big hand or something – was moving them all around, throwing them against each other to make them explode. I couldn't hear the sirens, but I saw the lights. Flashing. I was scared. I thought the city would be destroyed. The city of angels. Isn't that what they call it?

DAWSON: You could see all that from up here?

CATHY: Yes. From this house on Via el Sereno. My father bought this house because of the view. That's why we live up high, in the hills, so we can look down at the fire and see it but we never have to be in it. So he could be the night watchman.

DAWSON: I wish you didn't live so way up high. It's tough to make it up this hill on my bicycle.

CATHY: If you marry me, maybe my father will buy you a car.

DAWSON: A red one?

CATHY: Fire red.

DAWSON: Is that what you want? To be married?

CATHY: I want to go.

DAWSON: Where?

CATHY: (she points towards the window, taps the glass) Down there.

DAWSON: No, you don't.

CATHY: He said he would disinherit me.

DAWSON: If you marry me?

CATHY: (she nods) I would be on my own. Well…you and I would be.

DAWSON: Why would he do that to you?

CATHY: Because you're not Santa Barbara.

DAWSON: Well, you're not Carson.

CATHY: Take me there. I want to meet your mother. I've seen your sisters at school. The older one hates me.

DAWSON: Julie just thinks she's better than everyone else.

CATHY: Maybe she is. I mean, she's very pretty.

DAWSON: Sarah likes you.

CATHY: Sarah has never said a word to me. Not one word. She stares at the ground and walks on by.

DAWSON: She's younger. That's why.

CATHY: She seems sad to me.

DAWSON: She's not sad. She's just shy.

CATHY: No, I think she's sad. I think she likes being sad. Maybe she has a good time at it.

DAWSON: I could ask my mother if you could come to dinner one night.

CATHY: Is that when we'll tell them?

DAWSON: Tell them what?

CATHY: That we're getting married.

DAWSON: When did we decide to do that?

CATHY: It's the only way, Dawson.

DAWSON: It would never work. I'm not Santa Barbara, remember? You're Palos Verdes. The price is too high for you.

CATHY: Maybe he'll change his mind when I tell him how good you are at football. He might think you have a future then.

DAWSON: I do have a future.

CATHY: Really? Doing what?

DAWSON: I'm good at a lot of things.

CATHY: But you don't even surf.

DAWSON: Only because I have to work all the time.

CATHY: I wonder where my first job will be.

DAWSON: What do you want to do? For a career, I mean.

CATHY: I have no idea.

DAWSON: Not a single one?

CATHY: Nothing comes to mind.

DAWSON: I just wish you weren't sad all the time.

CATHY: I get sad when I think about the fighting…the riots. All the people who died.

DAWSON: Do you really think there are ghosts in this house?

CATHY: Too many to count.

DAWSON: Maybe that's why your mother takes her pills.

CATHY: No, she's keeping numb. She's just waiting. She wants a grandson. She'll be a better mother to him than I will be. He'll probably love her more, just to spite me.

DAWSON: I think you'll be a great mother.

CATHY: Only if I'm with you, Dawson.

DAWSON: What am I supposed to tell Barbara?

CATHY: Tell her that you're saving a life. You're teaching someone how to swim.

DAWSON: I'm no good at it. The only thing I know how to do is work. And play football.

CATHY: You wouldn't have come here unless –

DAWSON: I answered the phone.

CATHY: But do you regret it now?

DAWSON: (After a breath) I'm here, aren't I?

(CATHY turns to the window, reaches out for the city below but her fingertips stop at the glass.

Lights slowly fade to black.)

TIMOTHY BRAUN

Las Vegas Girl

ELLIS, father

SKIP, son

(The moonlight tower at Eastside Drive and Leland in Austin, TX 78704. Two men stand in the bright, artificial moonlight. Both men wear black. SKIP is between twenty and twenty five years in age. ELLIS is between thirty-five and forty years in age. Ellis rolls a joint, as Skip drinks from a bottle of wine.)

ELLIS: Where was everybody?

SKIP: She didn't know nobody.

ELLIS: No one from church?

SKIP: She stopped going a few years back. You and me are the only people she knew.

ELLIS: That's a shame. She used to be a real friendly girl.

SKIP: She was a friendly girl. But, she was fading toward the end and got mean. She couldn't fry an egg without help. She would mostly talk about your wedding. She had a chunk of the Berlin Wall the size of a cheeseburger, but had no clue how she got it.

ELLIS: I bought her that piece. From the TV.

SKIP: She kept it in a plastic ziplock bag. She painted the word "Mine" to the bag. She kept asking when you would be coming home from work towards the end.

ELLIS: What did you tell her?

SKIP: About what?

ELLIS: When I was coming home.

SKIP: I told her I didn't know. I told her you were busy. I didn't have the heart to tell her you found another woman.

ELLIS: I didn't find another woman.

SKIP: Then what do you call that girl you ran off with.

ELLIS: Don't make a scene.

SKIP: I'll make a scene when I damn well want to make a scene with you.

ELLIS: You think about your mother.

SKIP: Funny. You never did.

ELLIS: Skip.

SKIP: She tried to shoot herself with a squirrel rifle two years back. Spent two weeks at St. David's pullin' fragments out of her temple. Were you aware of that?

ELLIS: Yeah, I heard.

SKIP: Really? Never saw you come by. Never got no card or flowers or little stuffed animals. You do know that is what you are supposed to do when someone gets hurt, right? You send them stuff.

ELLIS: You knew where I was. It wasn't like I had a chance to visit.

SKIP: I did know where you were. Tampa, was it? With a

teenage girl.

ELLIS: Watch your mouth.

SKIP: I'm sorry. I didn't realize I was bothering you.

ELLIS: You ain't botherin' me.

SKIP: Clearly I am.

ELLIS: You are not botherin' me.

SKIP: How long are you gonna be in town?

ELLIS: What's it to you? You wanna go to the rodeo?

SKIP: If you're gonna be sleeping on my sofa…

ELLIS: I am not gonna stay on your sofa. I'm not interested in that.

SKIP: Where you gonna sleep? You don't have money, do you?

ELLIS: I'm not staying.

SKIP: How are you getting back to Florida?

ELLIS: I'm takin' a Greyhound in a few hours.

SKIP: And that's it.

ELLIS: Yeah. That's it.

SKIP: You're a real piece of work, Dad.

ELLIS: I don't think I've ever heard you call me that before.

SKIP: Dad? How could you? You split before I could walk.

ELLIS: That's not true. I saw you walk from the refrigerator to the sink when you were a kid. That was in our first apartment when we moved out here. When you were born. Didn't think I knew that, did you? I remember all sorts of things. In the fall, when the JCPenny's Christmas catalog would come, your mother would give you a blue ink pen and you'd mark all the toys you wanted. We couldn't afford any of 'em, but your mother loved to watch you look at that catalog.

(Silence.)

ELLIS: What do you do?

SKIP: What do you mean?

ELLIS: Work. What do you do?

SKIP: I do coat check at a hotel.

ELLIS: Which one?

SKIP: The Hyatt.

ELLIS: Don't know that one.

SKIP: It was built after your time.

ELLIS: A lot of stuff was built after I left. When your mother was with you, when we were in high school, in Michigan, I asked her what she wanted for her birthday. She said she wanted to see Siegfried and Roy. She liked tigers. I stole your grandfather's car, and when we got to Vegas, we decided to stay. I like the fact it never rained in the desert. And your grandfather let us keep the car. It all seemed perfect. You're mother wanted to be a Las Vegas girl.

SKIP: That's not how I heard it.

ELLIS: Yeah. I'm sure it's not. Your mother wanted to get a job as a showgirl, but all she could find was work as a waitress at Denny's. You got yourself a girl?

SKIP: Maybe.

ELLIS: Yeah, I bet. What does she do? Dance?

SKIP: She makes drinks at Expose.

ELLIS: She "makes drinks." You bein' honest with me?

SKIP: Sure. You still married to that wife of yours?

ELLIS: Sort of. She's with a shoe salesman now.

SKIP: Why did she leave you?

ELLIS: She didn't leave me. I let her go.

SKIP: Right.

ELLIS: Your mother still have that bird I bought her?

SKIP: Bird? No that finch died years ago. But she's had about a dozen since. She liked birds. They'd sing to her and listen to her and she'd put them in a cage so she always knew where they were. There was only one left when she died. I gave that one to a girl at Walmart. She works the photo lab. Are you embarrassed?

ELLIS: About what?

SKIP: Mom's birds?

ELLIS: Why?

SKIP: Because, you should be. An old woman, dying alone. With nothing but shit covered birds around her. It's humiliating.

ELLIS: Your mother wasn't that old. Why wasn't your girl at the funeral?

SKIP: She had to work.

ELLIS: She couldn't get off?

SKIP: She works paycheck to paycheck.

ELLIS: Your girl ever meet your mother?

SKIP: Why do you care?

ELLIS: I asked you a question.

SKIP: No. She didn't know Mom.

ELLIS: Why is that? Were you embarrassed by your crazy old mother? All alone with a bunch of shit covered birds?

SKIP: Don't call Mom crazy.

(Silence.)

ELLIS: When we first moved to Austin, we lived just up the road in that old green motel behind the gas station. Your mother and I would walk down here under the fake moon. It killed her when we left Vegas, but she sure did love this fake moon. Maybe we can see your girl after this. Get some tacos. There used to be a place just south of town where you could get oysters, as good as they get out here. We could get some oyster tacos.

SKIP: I really don't want that, Dad.

ELLIS: Don't call me that.

SKIP: What should I call you?

ELLIS: Ellis. Call me Ellis.

SKIP: Ellis. When was the first time you knew you didn't love Mom anymore?

ELLIS: I never stopped lovin' your mother. She was a fine specimen. She just asked too many questions. "Where you going? Where you been? Who you talkin' to on the phone?" She used to have the timing worked out between our apartment and my old job. So if I was five minutes late getting home from work, she'd ask trash like "who is she?" There never was no "she."

SKIP: Yes, there was.

ELLIS: No. Not back then. There was never another girl, until I left.

SKIP: When did you stop caring about me?

ELLIS: What makes you say that, Skip?

SKIP: Because you haven't looked at me once.

ELLIS: What do you want from me? Huh? Kid? Son. You want money? You want me to tell you I'm sorry about your mommy? I just got tired of listening to your mother. I'm sorry I wasn't around, but if I had stayed, I would've hung myself.

SKIP: All I ever wanted from you was a phone call.

ELLIS: I sent letters. I sent letters on your birthday and Christmas and Easter.

SKIP: Yeah, but all I wanted was a phone call. All I wanted to do was hear you.

ELLIS: You're hearin' me, ain't you?

SKIP: Yeah. Ellis. Smoke?

(ELLIS gives his son a joint. SKIP gives his father the wine.

They medicate in unison.)

ELLIS: Why don't you say somethin' about your mother?

SKIP: Mom would lay in bed and watch TV in the dark. She used to say it would relax her. She liked cartoons.

ELLIS: I didn't know that.

SKIP: Yeah. I bet you didn't. She used to say the birds were her best friends. Cause they would eat anything she cooked for them.

ELLIS: I can believe that. When you were four, and I guess that made your mother and me around twenty, your mother would make Kraft macaroni and cheese damn near every night for dinner cause that was the only thing you'd put in your mouth. And she'd mix in slices of cubed ham and that would be a real special thing for us.

SKIP: Us? I hate you.

ELLIS: You'd always pick out the ham with a spoon. And your mother would give the ham to me. We should buy some flowers for her.

SKIP: Screw you.

(Silence.)

SKIP: It's hot. We should get going. And I've got a bus to catch.

ELLIS: No. Not yet. Please.

(The two men stand under the fake moonlight smoking and drinking in unison.)

THE END

JASON VISCONTI

Dust and Doodads

MOTHER
DAUGHTER, 15
FATHER
BOY, 12

TIME Present

SCENE Daughter's bedroom

(The curtain rises on the disheveled DAUGHTER sitting in bed mumbling to herself. The MOTHER enters, carrying a purse and approaches her.)

MOTHER: Are you going crazy in my house again?

(The MOTHER sets her purse on the foot of the bed.)

DAUGHTER: Just trying to sort out some facts.

MOTHER: We've got to get you cleaned up for your father's party. The guests will be uncomfortable to see you in your pajamas.

DAUGHTER: Uncomfortable. Maybe if I take them off it will leave them anguished.

MOTHER: Don't talk about your body.

(The MOTHER leans over and smells her DAUGHTER.)

MOTHER: Are you wearing that hideous perfume?

DAUGHTER: Thank you for letting me know how horrible I

smell.

MOTHER: I would throw out your whole stash.

DAUGHTER: I'll leave it behind me.

MOTHER: But you don't get out of bed.

DAUGHTER: I mean literally behind me, tucked under this pillow.

MOTHER: Is that where you spend your life?

DAUGHTER: Everything I need is right here in this bed.

MOTHER: Now that's not party talk, dearie.

DAUGHTER: If I'm going to go in my kitchen, I'll go in my kitchen while the bastards are drinking. The last thing I'm worried about is being an eyesore.

MOTHER: Never mind that! You're not wearing any make-up! I wouldn't let you even stroll in front of the TV.

DAUGHTER: There's a gash in my face anyway. It's just that no one can see it.

MOTHER: I see it. You've got to close it up. It's far too dangerous.

DAUGHTER: You'll only see it for the moment. It will soon go away.

MOTHER: It's disgusting. It makes me feel I've neglected you.

DAUGHTER: It's healing, it's healing, it's healing.

MOTHER: My little girl's afraid.

DAUGHTER: Impossible!

MOTHER: Your cheeks are so pale. That can come from fear. Doll, just let me give you some make up.

DAUGHTER: No.

MOTHER: Why not?

DAUGHTER: I don't like the way it looks on you.

MOTHER: (points to herself) This, my dear, is the total woman. I could throw trash on my face and I would glow.

DAUGHTER: The total woman. All these years and I've never asked.

MOTHER: (forcing the words out) Brat…I use the best to show off these…these cheeks!

DAUGHTER: You think you know somebody until you find out their cosmetic secrets.

MOTHER: You should be prettying up your face right now instead of arguing with your mother.

DAUGHTER: For what? The drunks come in for Dad's birthday party every year. And for the record, I don't dress up unless there's someone waiting.

MOTHER: I can't promise that.

DAUGHTER: I wasn't implying.

MOTHER: All the men will know there's a woman hiding in her bedroom.

DAUGHTER: How? I'll keep the door locked. I'll keep my whispers low.

MOTHER: I'll tell them. And you'll deserve it, so shy to everyone else but your own Mother.

DAUGHTER: I won't get embarrassed. I refuse to.

MOTHER: And the big hefty men will applaud you in your absence, Mommy's little girl.

DAUGHTER: Those oddballs from Dad's job? I won't let them near me.

MOTHER: I'll make sure one doesn't peek in to say good night.

DAUGHTER: I would hate to have to nail this door shut.

MOTHER: I do cry a lot for my little girl. I want you to be happy, but I don't know how. Is there something in this tiny room you aren't showing me? A river in the closet? An island beneath that bed? Tell me, sweetheart, and then for today we can say at least good riddance.

DAUGHTER: It's all of that. It's all here.

MOTHER: What a child! She believes what she reasons must be so.

DAUGHTER: Can't you smell the grass, Mama? Taste the pollen in the air? Feel the sweet breeze by the ocean? I could never hide it. How could I hide it from you, Mama?

MOTHER: (obviously upset) Oh dear. (composes herself) Yes, I see it.

DAUGHTER: And what did that take you but a moment's thought? Now I think I'm ready for Daddy. That we've got that settled.

MOTHER: (having second thoughts) I think I've got the date confused...it's tomorrow, tomorrow's the party, never mind what I said.

DAUGHTER: Even if I wear the make-up, it won't make it daddy's birthday? Even if I twirl out of this room in your favorite dress?

MOTHER: It won't be your father's birthday for a long, long time.

DAUGHTER: And I was so hoping to impress everyone at the party. I guess I'll sleep in after all.

MOTHER: Maybe if you came out of your room for a moment to get a drink of water? It will do you good. You can wear that flowery dress.

DAUGHTER: The one I've been waiting to wear! If I drink my water!

MOTHER: I thought you'd be excited.

DAUGHTER: Sure I am. It's good water.

MOTHER: The finest.

DAUGHTER: And it's a good dress.

MOTHER: The best you have.

DAUGHTER: All the boys will love it.

MOTHER: I won't let them pick on you.

DAUGHTER: How gracious. And yourself? That smeared lipstick?

MOTHER: A true lady never overdoes it.

DAUGHTER: A true lady never needs it.

MOTHER: Actually, a true lady overdoes what she needs.

DAUGHTER: Am I a lady, Mama?

MOTHER: You have all the warning signals of a full-blown woman.

DAUGHTER: I know about woman. Am I a lady?

MOTHER: Decide that which way here for yourself. Are you?

DAUGHTER: A lady…what an interesting proposition. I'm just not sure. I might be, or I might not, I might be, or I might not…oh there I go, acting like a kid again. But it could be so fun to choose! Let the boys decide today as I drink my water in my beautiful flowery dress sashaying in front of the television with my own catwalk. (pause) Only for a moment, of course…as quickly as water goes down me.

MOTHER: So you don't need that river in your closet? That island underneath your bed? That sweet ocean breeze?

DAUGHTER: Do you need me to need them?

MOTHER: I want you to be happy.

DAUGHTER: (gathers herself) Do you actually think I believe these things? I don't. I imagine. The way I imagine this bed friendly company. It shouldn't hurt you. Why does it hurt you? I've found my companion.

MOTHER: I'll strip your bed down until he is gone.

DAUGHTER: Is that how you treat your daughter's heart?

MOTHER: Mattress and all.

DAUGHTER: You're not on my side if you want to destroy it.

MOTHER: I'll set your whole room on fire. Really get rid of the ghosts. You'd be out for many drinks of water after that.

DAUGHTER: I want you out of my room. You're insulting it. All of this talk.

MOTHER: I didn't know a room could get insulted, but just in case it can, let it take it.

DAUGHTER: No. It's out of hand. It demands you leave.

MOTHER: No.

DAUGHTER: No?

MOTHER: No. Let it suffer.

DAUGHTER: It really doesn't want to take any action you know.

MOTHER: What the hell do you mean?

DAUGHTER: It doesn't want to kill you. Not if it can help it.

MOTHER: This is what you've done to yourself? This is your young legacy?

DAUGHTER: It's really not up to me.

MOTHER: It's not up to either of us. You're going into the hospital again. Forget the party…party…if your Father ever knew!

DAUGHTER: Why don't you stick your head under my bed and see what happens? See if you want to come back.

MOTHER: Is this you when you imagine?

DAUGHTER: Some things I'm sure of.

MOTHER: It's because you're sick. And me throwing you headfirst into a crowd...

DAUGHTER: I think you're sick for not trying.

MOTHER: I know what's under your bed. Dust and doodads.

DAUGHTER: (ominously) Things have changed since last time you looked.

MOTHER: I'm so scared.

DAUGHTER: Don't be. The room is pleased. It just takes one offer.

MOTHER: I'm not scared about that...I'm scared for you.

DAUGHTER: If you let it be, I will be peaceful.

MOTHER: I want you dressed.

DAUGHTER: What's the matter, Mama, did I say a bad word?

MOTHER: You're startling me. And you will each time you say it.

DAUGHTER: (deliberately trying to irritate) Peaceful...peaceful ...peeecefullllll...

MOTHER: Don't do this to your Mother.

DAUGHTER: Perfectly adjusted.

MOTHER: Stop it.

DAUGHTER: The...dare I say, total woman?

MOTHER: (shaken) I'm gong to go under the bed. I'll go under. If I come back will you stop it? Please?

DAUGHTER: Just be careful. It can be overwhelming.

(The MOTHER bends down to look under the bed when a knock is heard on the door. FATHER enters.)

FATHER: Oh that's that island underneath the bed. I've seen it.

MOTHER: Seen it? There's nothing there.

FATHER: Yes there is. Go ahead. Look. Go ahead.

(The MOTHER crawls further beneath the bed.)

MOTHER: Dust and doodads.

FATHER: (to MOTHER) What are you afraid of? Loneliness can't be a nice trip?

(The MOTHER stands, brushes herself off.)

MOTHER: This is what you'll have for our daughter?

DAUGHTER: Nice trip nothing. Tonight it's supposed to rain on the coast.

MOTHER: (to FATHER) You have her giving weather reports.

FATHER: I didn't know it was going to rain.

DAUGHTER: I have an ear to the beach when I fall asleep at night.

MOTHER: What beach?

FATHER: Our daughter's beach. The rainy beach.

DAUGHTER: Now I'm ready for the storm.

MOTHER: (to FATHER) Is this how you celebrate your

birthday? By pretending with her? (to DAUGHTER) I want it to be real for you. But I can't.

DAUGHTER: I'll show you.

(The DAUGHTER hangs her head over the bed and looks under it.)

FATHER: (to MOTHER) Give it a real hard look. I'll close my eyes and wish you the best.

(The MOTHER crawls under the bed.)

MOTHER: There's nothing, dear. Nothing at all.

DAUGHTER: Don't you see it, Mama?

MOTHER: It's a picture…an unsigned postcard…

(The MOTHER crawls out from under the bed and stands holding a postcard. The DAUGHTER sits back up in bed.)

FATHER: And that's all there is.

DAUGHTER: It's the picture of someplace far away.

MOTHER: And all of this. I should tear it to shreds.

DAUGHTER: (disappointed) Mama…t's just a little bit of magic.

FATHER: (to MOTHER) I get these island scenes from the drugstore across the street. It's been nothing but a constant vacation for our precious little girl.

DAUGHTER: I can feel the picture underneath me when I sleep.

(Irate, the MOTHER takes a wallet out of her purse.)

MOTHER: I have a whole wallet full of pictures from all kinds of different places.

DAUGHTER: If you stare long enough at a picture...(double thinks what she wants to say)...well, you know what I mean. Anything can happen.

MOTHER: I can't believe this has been going on behind my back. I'll have that drugstore closed down. Selling merchandise for a sick woman.

DAUGHTER: Why am I sick? Because I can go to these places inside my head? What if you went there by foot? Would you be any more happy? Of course not. Someone send me a postcard and I'll just rub out the name. That is that.

MOTHER: (to FATHER) And you? You believe this kind of behavior is healthy?

FATHER: Idiot...you mentioned the word. Of course it's not healthy. None of us are. You're a grown woman and you just dug your way underneath your daughter's bed.

MOTHER: I was talked into...

FATHER: Never mind. You did it. You wanted to believe and now you can.

DAUGHTER: Now do you see why I can't join the party...why I'm content to be alone?

MOTHER: It's not the end of this. I'm getting you help.

DAUGHTER: (terrified) Daddy...the hospital?

FATHER: I don't think there's a cure for loneliness.

MOTHER: (puts her hands to her head) Maddening...I want to shut this out...

DAUGHTER: It seems my dear Mother has finally lost it.

FATHER: There are guests filing in expecting a party and just look what we've become.

DAUGHTER: I would like to be excused.

MOTHER: You want to leave?

DAUGHTER: Isn't that what you want?

MOTHER: After all this? To hop out of bed like it's nothing?

FATHER: Our daughter is welcome to get up and dance if she pleases.

DAUGHTER: Dance…I never get a picture of two people dancing.

MOTHER: You want to dance my sick, sick girl? Find a mirror and move your arms and legs.

DAUGHTER: A mirror…maybe that's what I'm missing. After all, you can see me, but I can't see me. I think I'll get one of those, you know, for good housekeeping.

FATHER: You look like you're ready for an entrance.

MOTHER: She can't go…they'll make fun of her. They'll call her crazy.

DAUGHTER: Sometimes crazy's all a person has.

FATHER: Give me your hand. I'll take you in.

DAUGHTER: I'm only going into another room.

MOTHER: Another room? A different world. I can't let it happen.

DAUGHTER: And you've so wanted me to wear that flowery dress.

MOTHER: That was when you were getting a drink of water.

DAUGHTER: A girl can wear her dress for any occasion. (pause) Mama, may I powder my face? I know there are things you can use if you're too plain of a girl.

MOTHER: Whose been calling you plain, dear?

DAUGHTER: It's just an idea of mine.

MOTHER: Sometimes ideas are right and sometimes they are wrong.

DAUGHTER: The whole city! Not one ugly face. I stare through that window jealous of the crowd.

FATHER: I want you to meet a boy that goes to school with your sister. He's out in the party right now. He's wondered for a long time why you never come out of your room. And he plays make-believe just like you...a twelve-year-old with an imaginary friend. Maybe his fantasies aren't as sophisticated as yours, but maybe in good time they will be.

MOTHER: (tense lipped) Do you really think she should be meeting this boy given her condition?

FATHER: And we should leave the room.

MOTHER: You're going to leave her alone with someone crazy?

FATHER: He's just a boy. A boy with a vivid imagination.

(FATHER exits.)

MOTHER: (to DAUGHTER) I want you to call me. Call me if things don't go well.

(BOY enters with FATHER.)

BOY: What's wrong with her?

MOTHER: See, he's insulting.

BOY: No, I mean, there's nothing wrong. It's just a girl lying in her bed.

DAUGHTER: My hero.

MOTHER: Careful what you call him it might stick.

BOY: (to DAUGHTER) Thank you.

MOTHER: (to BOY) Don't thank her it might stick.

FATHER: What a couple!

MOTHER: Don't, don't, don't! It might stick!

FATHER: Let's leave these two alone while you ponder over your horror.

(MOTHER and FATHER exit. The MOTHER looks back once before she leaves and sighs in despair.)

(BOY walks around the bed.)

BOY: You know you really have to get out of bed.

DAUGHTER: And who are you?

BOY: I'm the kid next door.

DAUGHTER: And now you're in my room.

BOY: I guess I am. (pause) Any resentments? After all you could say I'm an intruder.

DAUGHTER: Intruder? The first guest I have and look what he calls it. (pause) We can't be friends. With all our problems that would be too strange.

BOY: Why not? We share the same problem, which isn't even a problem since there's nothing wrong with pretending.

DAUGHTER: If you listen to my mother...

(BOY grabs DAUGHTER'S hands and holds them.)

BOY: I don't listen to mine.

DAUGHTER: Tell me something about your friend.

BOY: I can't.

DAUGHTER: Why not?

BOY: Right now, talking to you, he doesn't exist.

DAUGHTER: And I can't remember one postcard. Where have they gone?

BOY: Everything you have been holding on to has been replaced by something real.

DAUGHTER: I don't think I can manage real. I never could.

BOY: Do it slowly. Lift your body up muscle by muscle.

DAUGHTER: You mean off this bed?

BOY: Right off...but slowly.

DAUGHTER: It's been three years.

BOY: Three years of bracing for this moment.

DAUGHTER: I am cold.

BOY: You're bound to feel something after three years.

DAUGHTER: But my feet are warm. And I feel a tingle.

BOY: Now stand up! Stand!

(The DAUGHTER stands, wobbles, then corrects her balance.)

DAUGHTER: My head misses my pillow.

BOY: They've been laid on long enough. It's time to say goodbye.

DAUGHTER: How will I sleep? And when? And for how long?

BOY: Don't give those questions a second thought. You're finally free.

DAUGHTER: Now what do I do that I'm standing? What's left for me?

BOY: There are a million things.

DAUGHTER: My body feels tired.

BOY: For the both of us. But you must escape.

DAUGHTER: I have no one waiting for me in this world. No one bothered to care.

BOY: Why don't you visit one of those places in your pictures?

DAUGHTER: I do…everyday…

BOY: I mean for real.

DAUGHTER: I couldn't…

BOY: Why not?

DAUGHTER: I'm used to this room.

BOY: I'm sure there are other rooms in the Bahamas that look just like yours.

DAUGHTER: The beach. I'd be on the beach.

(The MOTHER and FATHER enter. They are shocked to see her standing.)

MOTHER: What are you doing? We called up the hospital. They'll be here in a few minutes.

DAUGHTER: Daddy, how could you let her!

FATHER: Be careful, dear. Do you need to sit down? I'm afraid I ruined you with postcards.

DAUGHTER: But I'm going to the beach! This time I really am.

MOTHER: You can't even swim.

DAUGHTER: Mother...

MOTHER: When the doctors come, you just explain everything that's wrong.

DAUGHTER: I can't walk this earth with strong enough legs!

MOTHER: I'll make sure they have you step into the ambulance. That should be good enough practice.

BOY: Call the ambulance off. I've already explained what she needs.

FATHER: You have no say here. Go back in the crowd.

BOY: I have more in common with her here than anyone.

DAUGHTER: (to BOY) Ride in the ambulance with me? Tell me about the beach? Until they knock me out with those drugs, keep my ears alert?

MOTHER: (to BOY) You can't get in. There's only room enough here for her mother...and her father, maybe.

FATHER: I blame it on myself...

MOTHER: Stop it. Everyone knows it's the girl's fault.

DAUGHTER: The girl...the girl...if I didn't know any better I would think that was a term of endearment.

FATHER: An ambulance! I see it through the window.

MOTHER: (suddenly) I'll call it off if you tell this boy go.

BOY: I'll go. Call it off.

DAUGHTER: No. He's with me now. He's my new companion.

MOTHER: Is he replacing the bed?

DAUGHTER: Forget it.

MOTHER: All those perfume bottles and pillows finally gone?

DAUGHTER: It's something separate...everything has changed.

MOTHER: They're coming upstairs by now. Will the boy go?

BOY: Why do you really want me gone? Are you too vain to admit your daughter's been found?

MOTHER: (to FATHER) Go downstairs and stall them. I want to have it out with this child alone.

(FATHER exits.)

MOTHER: Now…you see this is my daughter.

BOY: Yes, I do.

DAUGHTER: I do, too.

MOTHER: And she's my oldest daughter. My first born.

BOY: I remember.

MOTHER: And we don't want to be giving anyone false promises.

BOY: Yes.

MOTHER: You are still a boy.

BOY: A boy who can handle your little girl's dream.

MOTHER: This girl gets everything from school to food in her bed. She rarely even makes a cameo.

BOY: In the Bahamas, she'll be more than a postcard. She'll be picture perfect.

MOTHER: Is that where you're taking her? At age twelve?

BOY: With many other people and my father to chaperone.

MOTHER: Who are these people?

BOY: You might say admirers of your daughter.

MOTHER: But they don't know her?

BOY: They figure if the mother's a good woman, the daughter can't fall that far from the tree.

MOTHER: They think I'm a good woman?

DAUGHTER: The best. We were never enemies.

(The FATHER enters.)

FATHER: The ambulance just took down some information and left.

MOTHER: It's better they go. We wouldn't want to cause a spectacle.

DAUGHTER: Daddy…I'm going on a trip.

DADDY: To where, sweetheart?

DAUGHTER: To an island very far away.

CURTAIN

www.ingramcontent.com/pod-product-compliance
Lightning Source LLC
Chambersburg PA
CBHW030220170426
43194CB00007BA/806